Hyper-Calvinist Universal Salvation

Hyper-Calvinist Universal Salvation

The Systematic Theology of the Unchosen Saved by the Lake of Consuming Fire at the Eschaton

JEFF GRUPP

WIPF & STOCK · Eugene, Oregon

HYPER-CALVINIST UNIVERSAL SALVATION
The Systematic Theology of the Unchosen Saved by the Lake of Consuming Fire at the Eschaton

Copyright © 2024 Jeff Grupp. All rights reserved. Except for brief quotations in critical publications or reviews, no part of this book may be reproduced in any manner without prior written permission from the publisher. Write: Permissions, Wipf and Stock Publishers, 199 W. 8th Ave., Suite 3, Eugene, OR 97401.

Wipf & Stock
An Imprint of Wipf and Stock Publishers
199 W. 8th Ave., Suite 3
Eugene, OR 97401

www.wipfandstock.com

PAPERBACK ISBN: 978-1-6667-8958-4
HARDCOVER ISBN: 978-1-6667-8959-1
EBOOK ISBN: 978-1-6667-8960-7

05/24/24

All Scripture quotations are from the Authorized King James Version, unless otherwise indicated.

Dedicated to all humans—all chosen, all unchosen,
Who will all be in Christ's (GOD's) light in the afterlife forever

But we all, with open face beholding as in a glass the glory of the Lord, are changed into the same image from glory to glory, even as by the Spirit of the Lord.

—2 Corinthians 3:18

Neither is there any creature that is not manifest in his sight: but all things are naked and opened unto the eyes of him with whom we have to do.

—Hebrews 4:13

For it is written, As I live, saith the Lord, every knee shall bow to me, and every tongue shall confess to God.

—Romans 14:11

Contents

1. GOD (YHWH, Θεός) = Lake of Fire, Part 1 | 1
2. Hyper-Calvinist Universal Salvation: All Unchosen Saved by Immolation in Christ (GOD, YHWH, Θεός) at the Eschaton | 7
3. The Popular View of Hell Is Not Found in Scripture | 12
4. Scriptural Support for Hyper-Calvinist Universal Salvation, Part 1 | 14
5. Pre-Eschaton Annihilation | 18
6. The Two Stages of Salvation in Hyper-Calvinist Universal Salvation | 33
7. Eternal Punishment | 38
8. The Inevitable Gap of Annihilation Self-Nonexistence | 41
9. Lazarus and the Beggar (Luke 16) | 46
10. Scriptural Support for Hyper-Calvinist Universal Salvation, Part 2 | 50
11. Free Will and the Popular View of Hell | 63
12. GOD (YHWH, Θεός) = Lake of Fire, Part 2 | 68
13. The Twinkling of the Eye Is *before* the Earth Is Destroyed by Fire (Lake of Fire) | 86
14. Two Resurrections at Each End of the Thousand Years in a Day | 90
15. The Concept of Forever in Pre-Eschaton Underworldly Self-Nonexistence | 99

16	Passages That May Appear to Contradict Hyper-Calvinist Universal Salvation | 109
17	GOD Pulls Souls Out of the Vertical Infinity (Self-Nonexistence, Annihilation) | 116
18	GOD, Lake of Fire, is the Refiner's Fire | 121
19	All People Are Christ's Body, Omnitemporally Drawn to Him | 130
20	Why GOD Created Humans with Sin and Pain: A New Solution to the Problem of Pain and Evil | 135
21	The Hour Is Coming, and Now Is | 141

Bibliography | 145

Bibliography | 147

Bibliography | 153

1

GOD (YHWH, Θεός) = Lake of Fire, Part 1

IN THE GOSPEL OF John, we witness something rather peculiar: what appears to be a direct contradiction: in chapter 3, verse 17, we appear to be told that nobody will be condemned, and in verse 18 we appear to be told that many are condemned:

> 17 For God sent not his Son into the world to condemn the world; but that the world through him might be saved. 18 He that believeth on him is not condemned: but he that believeth not is condemned already, because he hath not believed in the name of the only begotten Son of God. (John 3:17–18)

As we will see, there are verses that glut Scripture which contain each of these two opposing claims: that there are some who are condemned, and that there will not be any condemned. So, is there a blatant contradiction in the Bible?

This book presents a novel evangelical systematic theology, which I call *Hyper-Calvinist universal salvation*, that involves the thesis, derived from the plainest reading of Scripture, that GOD reverses the condemnation of all the condemned at the Eschaton. Hyper-Calvinist universal salvation is a theology where GOD saves *all* the unchosen, starting, Scripture tells us, at his Descension at the Eschaton. Starting at that event, he burns away the corruption and flesh of the condemned when he saves their spirit at the Eschaton (see 1 Cor 5:5, for example), in the Fire of his Being. In Scripture, this Fire of his Being refers to who and what GOD is, which is the one who saves by immolation (see 1 Cor 3:12–15, to give an initial example), which is involved in what GOD's names are, such as the Consuming Fire. In this book, I will also find that GOD is not just the Consuming Fire, but also the

Hyper-Calvinist Universal Salvation

Lake of Fire, and the Baptism of Fire. I will also use the term *Eschaton Fire* to refer to GOD. So, there is no contradiction between John 3:17 and 3:18, since condemnation, on the one hand, and the omnisalvation of humanity, on the other, do not coincide in time; they are stages of salvation, as we will discover below.

Scripture tells us that before the Eschaton, men are blinded from understanding Scripture (see Eccl 3:11 and 11:5; Mark 4:11–12; Zeph 1:17; John 12:40; 2 Cor 4:3–4; Isa 25:7; John 9:39, 1 Cor 1:18; Isa 55:8, among many other passages that could be cited), and, *ipso facto*, there can only still be big discoveries waiting to be found through evangelical and inerrantist systematic analysis of the Bible. And what I call Hyper-Calvinist universal salvation involves a few such discoveries. It involves a novel eschatology uncovered from Scripture, where in the future, GOD will save all condemned and unchosen human souls that were ever created, at the Eschaton, by immolating them in his Consuming Fire. Perhaps this has not been discovered in evangelical and inerrantist readings of Scripture hitherto because the mysterious concept of the Lake of Fire, that is cited late in the book of Revelation, has been falsely believed to be identical to the traditional notion of hell. According to that popular (and non-biblical) view of hell, the GOD of perfect forgiveness and love supposedly, and inconceivably, burns multitudes of unchosen people in hellfire *forever*, via unfathomable torture. I believe it is safe to say that Hitler, for example, probably would have loved to have such torture methods at his disposal. But there is no scripture that indicates GOD ever burns people in hell, and the Lake of Fire is not a description of hell or any part of the underworld, but rather, the Lake of Fire is another name *for GOD*, the Consuming Fire, as I will reveal in this chapter.

In my experience, when people seek to "verify" that hell is scriptural, and that the concept GOD casting people into hell to be tortured unthinkably in fire forever is scriptural, they cite the Lake of Fire verses in Revelation 20 and 21. But in those verses, "hell" is never equated with the Lake of Fire, there is no underworldly quality whatsoever to the Lake of Fire, and the Lake of Fire has no resemblance to the popular view of hell. Instead, the Lake of Fire has qualities that are only possessed by *GOD*, such as how when immersed within the Lake of Fire, death and hell *cease to exist* (see Rev 20:14[1]—multiple chapters in this book are dedicating to this

---

1. In the newer translations, the word "Hades" is used, the realm of death sleep. And the 1550 Textus Receptus uses "Hades" (αδης), as do the newer translations. The KJV, however, translates αδης as "hell." Hell, therefore, in that context, would be taken as being an aspect of Hades.

GOD (YHWH, Θεός) = Lake of Fire, Part 1

topic). GOD is the only one who ends death—but the Lake of Fire does as well (Rev 20:14), and therefore the Lake of Fire is another name for GOD, inside of which most people are burned at the Eschaton, saved by Fire (1 Cor 3:15, Exod 12:10–13). This understanding of the Eschaton unveils an elegant Hyper-Calvinistic systematic theology throughout Scripture, where the unchosen/condemned have their condemnation reversed, healed, by the GOD of infinite love, at the Eschaton.

This theology stems from the attempt to carry out a literalist (or perhaps better stated as a hyper-literalist) account of Scripture, by reading the Bible the way a poor man would, or a man who does not have seminary education. According to this sort of a minimally interpretive reading of Scripture, when one reads any verse or passage, it is taken to mean *just what it says*, as I often say in day-to-day ministry. If Scripture says GOD will soon burn the heavens and the earth with Fire, for example, then that is deemed to be a literal event that is imminent. Putting all of this in different words: attempting the plainest, most simplistic reading of Scripture—like a simpleton would—and developing a metaphysics of reality, and a systematic theology, *from that* sort of just-take-it-for-what-it-says reading, reveals a wholly logical, elegant, brilliantly consistent systematic theology, that avoids many, or perhaps *all*, of the paradoxes, conflicts, and contradictions so widely (but erroneously) believed to exist in the Bible, and which reveals how GOD saves *all* people via his perfect love. This sort of hyper-literalist reading of Scripture is in-line with the dictation view of Scripture, where it is held that GOD alone wrote the Bible, GOD moved Paul's pen, so to speak. This is a stronger position than the inspired view, where humans are viewed as using their volition to participate in the creation of GOD's Word. But if that were the case, then beings who were liars (humans, that is, see Rom 3:4, Ps 116:11), would be the free-willed creators of Scripture, where Scripture would then contain lies. This book is, however, an evangelical systematic theology, where GOD's dictation is viewed as the only possibility for how GOD's Word was written, since GOD is the Creator of all things, and apart from him we can do nothing (John 15:5).

With this sort of reading of Scripture, and on my estimation from years of reading Scripture, the most widely discussed concept in the Bible is the Eschaton, at which GOD will *save all the unchosen*, the unsaved, at the end of the world, in his Fire, to live with Christ (GOD) in the afterlife forever. The dominating view of eschatology, that has monopolized Christianity since the early days of the church, has been the view that the love-GOD

(YHWH, Θεός) (1 John 4:7–8) created scores of people just to consciously torture them in hell-fire forever. But that view does not exist in Scripture, and the opposite view gluts the pages of the Bible, for example:

> 20 and, having made peace through the blood of his cross, by him *to reconcile all things unto himself*,[2] by him, I say, whether they be things in earth, or things in heaven. 21 And you, that were sometime alienated and enemies in your mind by wicked works, *yet now hath he reconciled* 22 in the body of his flesh through death, to present you holy and unblameable and unreproveable in his sight. (Col 1:20–22)

I have been told that some of the findings I come to in this book apparently have not been noticed previously, despite their being in plain sight in Scripture. I believe the most significant discovery in this book is that the Lake of Fire is not a description of a hell, but rather is, scripturally speaking, *identical to* GOD (YHWH, Θεός), the *Consuming Fire* (Heb 12:29), where *all* humans will see him as the Consuming Fire at the Eschaton (Isa 40:5, Luke 3:6, Mark 9:49). There are at least two quite robust scriptural evidences for this position, that the Lake of Fire is the Consuming Fire (GOD).

First, the Lake of Fire, like GOD, transcends all things. The concept of the Lake of Fire found late in the book of Revelation has been confused into being imagined to be either *identical to* the traditional, popular view of hell, or as being some sort of hell-like scenario that GOD uses after the heavens and earth pass away to put people in, in order to torture people forever. Careful analysis of Scripture will show us that those views are not correct, since (1) at the Eschaton there is an end to all things (1 Pet 4:7; Mark 13:3; Matt 24:35), where that end specifically comes by Fire (2 Pet 3:7; Mal 4:1; Luke 12:49; 2 Pet 3:12), and where the underworld regions, such as hell, Hades, etc., would have to be included in those things that come to an end. And since, (2) it is specifically by Fire *of GOD* (Isa 66:15; 2 Pet 3:7, 12), an immolating of everything inside of GOD, that ends all things—as if all things will be deeply immersed *inside of* an ocean of Fire at the end of the world (immersed in a Lake of Fire during the Eschaton) that eradicates all things, including the underworlds, such as hell and Hades (for example, see Rev 20:14). So, at the Eschaton, all things fade away (perhaps primarily,

---

2. I will freely italicize parts of Scripture passages quoted in this book that illustrate Hyper-Calvinist universal salvation. With few exceptions, the italicizing used is my emphasis, but the reader should consult Scripture in passages cited in this book if they want to be sure.

GOD (YHWH, Θεός) = Lake of Fire, Part 1

or even exclusively, via immolation inside of the Lake of Fire/GOD), but the Lake of Fire *nevertheless exists*. This would mean that the Eschaton Fire, that immerses and ends all things, like an ocean or lake (Lake of Fire), *is beyond all things*—it *exists* when all things do not. For that reason, the Lake of Fire transcends all things—just like GOD does (see Phil 4:7, and 1 Pet 4:7)—as a higher order of reality (or better stated: as a *post-reality*), at the *end* of all things. The Fire at the end, the Lake of Fire, is not an ordinary fire, but rather is a Fire that exists after everything has passed away. So, this world- and reality-ending Fire is beyond all things, just as GOD is beyond all things, and the Eschaton Fire at the end of the world, this ocean of Fire (Lake of Fire), is therefore described in the way GOD is described: a Consuming Fire that ends, transcends, and, as we will see, restores all things (Acts 3:21).[3]

Secondly, and perhaps more powerfully, this world-ending Lake of Eschaton Fire, unhidden at the end, is revealed in Scripture as having the *very same* qualities that only GOD (YHWH, Θεός) can have, in another, seemingly more incisive, way. Specifically, *both* GOD *and* the Lake of Fire are described *as ending death* in Scripture (compare Rev 20:14 and Isa 25:8). If GOD is the only one who ends death, and if the Lake of Fire ends all death, then the Lake of Fire and GOD can only be *identical*: the Lake of Fire is described in Scripture as identical to GOD. And further, GOD, the Lake of Fire, comes at the Eschaton with Fire, since he is the Consuming Fire, and we will find in chapters below that GOD can be shown to be *identical to*, *equal to*, the Eschaton Fire, which Scripture tells us will save all the condemned. In this book, we will find that Lake of Fire is merely another name for the Eschaton Fire, or Consuming Fire, which is GOD (Jesus the Christ, YHWH, Θεός). So, we will find that Scripture indicates that the trajectory of the condemned human though time is as follows: live in the physical body as a living soul, then after body death the unchosen soul is brought to the Eschaton, wherein the unchosen human is resurrected (awakened, brought back into existence), to be put into the Lake of Fire (immolation in

---

3. Scripture says that at the Eschaton, there is an *end* to all things (1 Pet 4:7), *and* that there will be a reconciliation of all things to him (Acts 3:21). A theme in this book is that at the Eschaton, GOD (Jesus, YHWH, Θεός) ends all things, *and* makes all things new (Rev 21:5; also see Isa 43:18–19; 2 Cor 5:17). Putting these verses together indicates that reality will be ended by the Fire of GOD (Lake of Fire, Consuming Fire) at the Eschaton, which is the end of all things (1 Pet 4:7), and then re-created in a "post-reality," after the heavens and the earth have been burned away, perhaps roughly described as a spirit-reality, where some, or all, people, will be equal to angels (Luke 20:36 KJV wording only).

Hyper-Calvinist Universal Salvation

GOD), in order to burn away the flesh and corruption, to thus be saved in Christ, forever, via GOD-immolation at the Eschaton.

Another finding in this book, which has been excluded from the dominating view since the time of the early church, and thus not widely discussed since then, is that GOD (whom I refer to as the Eschaton Fire) will save *all condemned and unchosen* human souls that were ever created for our cosmos, at the Eschaton, specifically *by revealing himself* (see 1 John 3:2), during his Descension, revealing himself as ecstatic Fire (Ezek 8:2–4; Isa 13:8; Acts 2, especially verses 3–4 and 15; Deut 4:36; Dan 7:7-9; Ps 16:11): purifying Baptism of Fire of the Eschaton (Lake of Fire). So, this is a *universalist* (universal salvation) position, and the Hyper-Calvinist universal salvation theology of this book I hope can be a step *forward* (that is, more scripturally sound) in the development of this theology.

So, a quite new and different theological model, and picture of the Christian Creator GOD, emerges out of Scripture from this literalist approach to Scripture. It is a view where GOD is lovingly coinhering himself with, and atoning himself with (see Rom 5:11), all his creatures (humans), as he restores all things (Acts 3:21). This is an analytic systematic theology where every person we ever see or talk to in our lives, and any and every person we can know, will be saved (atoned with GOD), and nothing can or will stop this.

2

Hyper-Calvinist Universal Salvation

All Unchosen Saved by Immolation in Christ (GOD, YHWH, Θεός) at the Eschaton

HYPER-CALVINIST UNIVERSAL SALVATION CAN be defined as follows:

> In the present, before the Eschaton, there are *both* saved and condemned people (there are both chosen and unchosen people). At the Eschaton, the LORD will descend in full revealing, where all humans and all flesh will see him together (Isa 40:5; Joel 2:28; Rev 1:7), as he is (1 John 3:2). The salvation of the condemned starts at this point. *After* the Descension, he will continue to be revealed as Fire, as the Consuming Lake of Fire that ends all things. All things will be immersed within, and immolated by, GOD's Fire. The immolation in the Fire of GOD leads to *all* the unchosen and unsaved—including murderers, oppressors, and any and all of the most hated criminals—having their flesh destroyed, wherein their spirit is saved (1 Cor 3:12–15; 5:5; Exod 12:10–13; 1 Tim 2:3–4 KJV wording) and made new, thus being given unearned (Rom 4:6) supernatural salvation.[1]

---

1. The Hyper-Calvinist universal salvation of this book is distinct from Augustinian universalism (which is discussed in Crisp, *Deviant Calvinism*, chapter 4), which sometimes is considered a "Calvinist universalism." The evangelical Hyper-Calvinist universal salvation contained in this book has no similarities to Augustinian universalism.

Hyper-Calvinism is a little discussed antinomian (Toon, *Emergence of Hyper-Calvinism*, 145) and extreme supralapsarian (Toon, 82) theology established largely by nonconformist preachers in England in the later 1600s to the mid 1700s. Hyper-Calvinism has been largely unstudied and misunderstood. It rejects free will, holding that divine revelation alone saves the human (Toon, 104–5). In Hyper-Calvinism, the believer knows they are elect not by their free will choice to believe, but rather, by feeling GOD

Hyper-Calvinist Universal Salvation

According to Hyper-Calvinist universal salvation, it is claimed that Scripture shows that we humans, in this physical realm, live in a reality that aligns with some type of extreme five-point Calvinism (i.e., a "more rigid form of Calvinism, Hyper-Calvinism," Toon, *Hyper-Calvinism*, 66), but with a doctrinal element added, that was missing from original Hyper-Calvinism in British nonconformity, which is: according to Scripture, the unchosen *are all saved* by the revealing of GOD-Christ the Consuming Fire at the Eschaton. Unlike other types of Christian universal salvation, there *is* a hell in Hyper-Calvinist universal salvation, since that is what Scripture indicates (see Luke 10:15 and Rev 20:13 both in KJV wording)—though, and as we will see below, Scripture does not state that any people are actually ever burning, or tortured in hell, as other scholars before me have noted. Also, as Scripture indicates, hell, and all regions and dimensions of the underworld, cease to exist at the Eschaton (discussed below). For unknown reasons, this theology of Hyper-Calvinist universal salvation—where the Fire of GOD *is* the Eschaton (the Lake of Fire), the Consuming Fire, *saving* all the unsaved—has apparently been missed by theologians hitherto, which is surprising (at least to me), since copious Scripture will be presented below to back up the systematic theology of Hyper-Calvinist universal salvation presented in this book.

To give some initial scriptural support here at the outset, consider the follow passages, which can serve to give to examples of Hyper-Calvinist universal salvation. Here is the first:

(via introspection) in their soul (Toon, 104–5, 145)—whereby such awareness of GOD would lead to eruptions of the ecstatic presence of GOD (Acts 2:23). Hyper-Calvinists held to an absolute omnicausality (there is only one cause of all things, and that cause is GOD-Christ) and hyper-sovereignty of GOD. Hyper-Calvinism emphasizes an absolutely literalist reading of Scripture (Toon, 79), an emphasis on GOD's omnipresence revealed throughout nature (Toon, 104), and it involves an emphasis in ministering less to the non-elect, and to a greater extent to the elect (Toon, 80). Scripture appears to indicate that the elect tend to be the poor, or even the poorest (see Luke 6:20, for example). Therefore, a true Hyper-Calvinism should lead to emphasis on serving and preaching to the poorest (just as Jesus also emphasized): the diseased, handicap, the oppressed, the prisoners, blind, maimed (see Luke 14:12–15). Taken to its logical conclusion, Hyper-Calvinism would lead the Hyper-Calvinist to commune primarily with the poor (the elect), or even animals (see Ps 150:6 and Mark 16:15), perhaps in the way of Francis of Assisi and other pre-Reformation mendicants and radicals.

Hyper-Calvinist Universal Salvation

For as in Adam *all die*, even so in Christ *shall all* be made alive.[2,3]
(1 Cor 15:22)

Notice how this verse refers to *all* people being saved, but the verse involves a *pointing into the future*, where the universal salvation happens at some *future* point, as indicated by the "shall be" (KJV, ESV) or "will be" (NIV, NRSV, NASB) in the verse. Each of these translations agree about universal salvation, *and* that this universal salvation will happen *in the future*. There are still condemned people, presently, but at the Eschaton, this will be reversed, and all people who were ever created for our cosmos, will be changed, given supernatural salvation, to have selves which can no longer sin. These themes are continued in the next two verses after 15:22, where *all people* referred to in 15:22 are Christ's, and where such universal salvation occurs specifically in the future, and at his Eschaton:

2. I believe many will claim that verses like this *appear to be* universalist, but nevertheless universalism *does not* exist, since humans, by their free will, can choose to reject GOD, which it is often claimed the majority of people *do*, and thus universalism does not exist. But I will claim, including in a footnote late in the book, that human free will is not found in the Bible, it is heretical and contradictory (i.e., impossible), and therefore cannot exist.

3. In this verse, it can be shown that "made alive" is a reference to salvation, and therefore salvation *for all*. I say this because other places in Scripture refer to salvation as "life," such as Matt 7:14: "because strait is the gate, and narrow is the way, which leadeth unto life, and few there be that find it." In Matt 7:13–14 there is a dichotomy, life or not life, where in Matt 7:13, the narrow way is that of *destruction*, which is a reference to *annihilation*, a topic Jesus revisits elsewhere in the Gospels (see discussion of pre-Eschaton annihilationism in a chapter below). Therefore, the opposite of the annihilation/destruction of Matt 7:13 is life, as discussed in 7:14. The dichotomy presented in Matthew 7:13–14 is annihilation versus salvation, where salvation is life (7:14). This would point to life in Jesus, or being "made alive" in him (as 1 Cor 15:22 also discusses), *as being salvation*. Also, and perhaps even more straightforwardly, Jesus is identical to salvation (Luke 2:25–30), and in John 14:6, he says Jesus is life. Therefore, salvation (Jesus) is life. And consider Romans 5:18, a thoroughgoing universalist verse:

> Therefore as by the offence of one judgment came upon all men to condemnation; even so by the righteousness of one the free gift came upon *all* men unto justification of *life*.

This verse maintains that the *free gift* (which is salvation; Rom 6:23: "For the wages of sin is death; but the gift of God is *eternal life* through Jesus Christ our Lord") is the reason or explanation ("justification") for *life*. The "free gift," Jesus, who is salvation, eternal *life*, is referred to in Romans 5:15 as "the grace of God . . . which is by one man, Jesus Christ." According to John 4:10, the gift of GOD is *living* water.

For these reasons, 1 Corinthians 15:22 is referring to salvation as being "made alive," which is the reversal of the death in Adam.

Hyper-Calvinist Universal Salvation

> 23 But every man in his own order: Christ the firstfruits; *afterward they that are Christ's at his coming.* 24 *Then cometh the end*, when he shall have delivered up the kingdom to God, even the Father; when he shall have put down all rule and all authority and power. (1 Cor 15:23–24)

Next, consider 2 Peter:

> 6 whereby the world that then was, being overflowed with water, perished: 7 but the heavens and the earth, which are now, by the same word are kept in store, *reserved unto fire* against the day of judgment and perdition of ungodly men. 8 But, beloved, be not ignorant of this one thing, that one day is with the Lord as a thousand years, and a thousand years as one day. 9 The Lord is not slack concerning his promise, as some men count slackness; but is longsuffering to us-ward, not willing that any should perish, but that all should[4] come to repentance. (2 Pet 3:6–9)

This passage mentions an ocean of fire (Lake of Fire), as the second flood, that consumes everything (verses 6 and 7), completely overwhelming the physical reality, and all of the heavens, bringing the end of all things (1 Pet 4:7; Matt 24:35). And the passage indicates that the Fire was and is reserved for ungodly men, which can only definitively be *all* men (see Rom 3:10): *GOD seeks all men, unwilling to let any perish* (verse 9). It seems safe to say that the context of this passage is the burning in the Fire of GOD (Lake of Fire) of all people, but the passage concludes with GOD not being willing that any should perish. The only way those seemingly incompatible and opposite concepts—that all are burned, and that none will perish—can be reconciled and juxtaposed is to conclude that the burned are *saved* in association with the burning and therefore with the Fire (see 1 Cor 3:14–15; Exod 12:10–13). And consider another initial scriptural example of Hyper-Calvinist universal salvation:

> 3 For this is good and acceptable in the sight of God our Saviour; 4 Who will have *all* men *to be* saved, and to come unto the knowledge of the truth. (1 Tim 2:3-4)

And consider one more example, to see Hyper-Calvinist universal salvation in the pages of Scripture:

> 8 Therefore wait ye upon me, saith the LORD, until the day that I rise up to the prey: for my determination is to gather the nations,

---

4. "Should come to" is the Greek χωρῆσαι, "to come."

that I may assemble the kingdoms, to pour upon them mine indignation, even all my fierce anger: *for all the earth shall be devoured with the fire of my jealousy.* 9 For then will I turn to the people a pure language, that they may *all* call upon the name of the LORD, to serve him with one consent. (Zeph 3:8–9)

As can be seen to this point, Hyper-Calvinist universal salvation is not in line with contemporary and popular Christian theological inventions. While exploring Hyper-Calvinist universal salvation, in this book we will see that many of the contemporary pop-theological concepts are not scriptural, perhaps drawing to mind a passage of prophecy about being in a time where sound doctrine is not endured (see 2 Tim 4:3–4). The reader may be in disbelief that Hyper-Calvinist universal salvation could be so plainly scriptural, yet not discovered by the famous theologians, but that is what I will show in this book. In other words, I will show that theology, worldwide, has involved false eschatologies, where the specific *falsehood* is the view that the majority of souls GOD creates are put, by him, into an inescapable and unending torture of fire, to be consciously tortured in hell in unthinkable terror, with literally no end, with no chance of cessation of the unthinkable torture. Nothing even remotely similar to these sorts of concepts are found via the aforementioned literalist interpretation of Scripture, and we will find that roughly the *opposite* metaphysics of reality is found in Scripture.

3

The Popular View of Hell Is Not Found in Scripture

I HAVE FOUND THAT there are few things that deter people away from Christianity more than the cruelty of the popular and traditional view of hell, supposedly allowed and/or carried out by GOD. That view may be popular in brick-and-mortar churches, but it is specifically the view not found in Scripture. The popular and traditional view of hell can be summed up as follows.

> Popular view of hell (non-scriptural): The all-loving Creator God creates most people for little more than to put them into difficult lives, with little if any awareness of God, while they live in the physical domain, and after that, God tortures most of them forever, in *fully conscious*, deepest, and most unfathomable inner terror, pain, horror, and burning, in screaming pain, with not the slightest chance of *ever* letting up on this horrific situation, for a mathematical infinity of time everlastingly, all merely because a person, in their less-than-supernatural level of intelligence, allegedly did not make the correct free will choice, of their own accord (a choice not originating from the Creator of all, but rather from the autonomy of the corrupted human self), while living in the physical domain.

There is no Scripture that supports anything like this sort of a theology.[1]

---

1. If this is correct, that nothing like this view exists in Scripture, and the correct (scriptural) view involves roughly the opposite sort of theology (e.g., GOD saves *all* by Fire, etc.), then, scripturally speaking, this popular and traditional view of hell would be in line with what Scripture calls "doctrines of devils" of the end times (1 Tim 4:1).

The Popular View of Hell Is Not Found in Scripture

My career is in jail ministry, and this popular, traditional view of hell is the principal objection and source of confusion about Christianity that I see amongst the many jail inmates. In other words, something that is not even in Scripture (the popular and traditional view of hell), is the primary concept I see confusing the believers I encounter daily in ministry, and even leading some of them to stray from the faith due to the confusion. It is also a primary objection that I see opposers to Christianity use to doubt and/or attack Christianity. And it is the primary objection I see that turns existing believers in Christ away from GOD and into agnosticism or atheism. The opposers claim that Christianity is absurd, since a maximally wonderful and all-loving GOD, a GOD that is the greatest conceivable Being (Heb 6:13), the infinite Spirit, who is only capable of infinite greatness, cannot be the same Being that creates multitudes of beings only to torment them, without any end, in a mathematical infinity of unending time, with torture so horrific that you or I could not even fathom. From what I can tell, this objection is logically flawless, and it reveals a contradiction in contemporary popular theology (in the popular and traditional view of hell, that is), which has strayed from the pure and infinite logic of Scripture. On the simpleton's literalist reading of Scripture, GOD is not a GOD of contradiction, but of perfect logic, and what if the opposers merely have a sound objection: how can needless, infinitely cruel terror and torture be created by, and originate from, GOD, the Being of infinite love? I have heard jail inmates say that they would not even wish that terror and torture on their worst enemy, so how could the GOD of *infinite love and kindness* desire that, or even have the capacity to conceptualize (see Hab 1:13) and create anything like *that*? How could the most horrific imaginable torture come from *infinite* love? This is like saying infinite, pure dryness comes only from maximum wetness, which is a logical, analytical contradiction. If the popular view of hell were correct, Christianity would be contradictory and therefore not real.

I find it revealing how a view such as the popular view of hell can be ubiquitously believed in, as if it were a foundational issue in Christianity, but where it is actually not in Scripture, and therefore it is *mistakenly* believed to be a foundational issue in Christianity. I will continue to discuss below how there are no verses or passages anywhere in Scripture that discuss a fiery underworld burning some or all the unchosen without any end, and how the mainstream view of hell does not exist in Scripture, which can only disclose that at least some of the basic tenets of contemporary worldwide pop theology are *wrong*.

4

Scriptural Support for Hyper-Calvinist Universal Salvation, Part 1

CONSIDER THESE ADDITIONAL VERSES and passages which verify Hyper-Calvinist universal salvation:

> For it is written, As I live, saith the Lord, *every* knee *shall* bow to me, and *every tongue shall confess*[1] to God. So then *every one of*

1. We can see in other Scripture that confessing the Name is what is done by one who is saved or being saved, which would indicate that if *all* are to confess, then all are to be forgiven (1 John 2:2; John 1:29; and KJV wording for Mark 3:28), and all saved:

> That if thou shalt confess with thy mouth the Lord Jesus, and shalt believe in thine heart that God hath raised him from the dead, thou shalt be saved. For with the heart man believeth unto righteousness; and with the mouth confession is made unto salvation. (Rom 10:9–10)

> Hereby know ye the Spirit of God: Every spirit that confesseth that Jesus Christ is come in the flesh is of God: and every spirit that confesseth not that Jesus Christ is come in the flesh is not of God: and this is that spirit of antichrist, whereof ye have heard that it should come; and even now already is it in the world. (1 John 4:2–3)

> When heaven is shut up, and there is no rain, because they have sinned against thee; if they pray toward this place, and confess thy name, and turn from their sin, when thou afflictest them: then hear thou in heaven, and forgive the sin of thy servants, and of thy people Israel, that thou teach them the good way wherein they should walk, and give rain upon thy land, which thou hast given to thy people for an inheritance. (1 Kgs 8:35–36)

We can also see similar actions with the tongue regarding salvation. For example, Joel 2:32 states that "whosoever shall *call on* the name of the Lord shall be delivered." Also see 1 John 4:15 and 2 John 1:7.

Scriptural Support for Hyper-Calvinist Universal Salvation, Part 1

us shall give account of himself to God. Let us not therefore judge one another any more: but judge this rather, that no man put a stumblingblock or an occasion to fall in his brother's way.[2] (Rom 14:11–13)

And *all* flesh *shall* know[3] that I the LORD am thy Saviour and thy Redeemer. (Isa 49:26)

---

2. This same message of every knee bowing also appears in Phil 2:10–11 and Isa 45:23.

> That at the name of Jesus every knee should bow, of things in heaven, and things in earth, and things under the earth; and that every tongue should confess that Jesus Christ is Lord, to the glory of God the Father. (Phil 2:10–11)

Regarding this verse in Philippians, and discussing what seems to be the blatant universalism of "every knee shall bow," MacDonald writes:

> First, this acknowledgement of Christ is universal. Paul emphasizes that there are no exceptions by expanding the Old Testament text "every knee will bow" with the words *"in heaven and on earth and under the earth."* This is going considerably further than the Isaiah text. In Isaiah only the living were in mind. All the survivors of the nations would bow, but the dead were dead. Not so here. Even those "under the earth," that is to say, the dead, will bow. So the picture is of every single individual who has ever lived acknowledging the rule of Christ. This much is not terribly controversial amongst commentators. Second, this vision is of universal salvation. It is common to suggest that, although all creatures here will bow the knee, some will be forced to do so against their will prior to being damned. (MacDonald, *Evangelical Universalist*, 98)

MacDonald, interestingly, hints at the conflict that the Bible's message of universal salvation has with supposed *human free will choice*—a term and concept that does not appear anywhere in Scripture, nor do any of its cognates. In another footnote below, I discuss the *lack* of need of any so-called free will choice in Hyper-Calvinist universal salvation. Hyper-Calvinist universal salvation, therefore, is a theology that does not contain or include the widely discussed conflict between free will choice and GOD's sovereignty.

And lastly, some may maintain that the context of Romans 14 is about Paul's exhortation to both weak and strong in Roman churches to stop judging one another regarding food, and it is not about humanity's eternal destiny. I maintain that such a view is partial, incomplete, since at Rom 14:10b–14:11a, we see a shift from talking about the judging over food to a broader scope, moving to a broader discussion, of standing before the judgment seat of Christ. The topic shifts to the judgment seat, an Eschaton event, wherein which we are told that every knee *shall* bow, every tongue confess, and thereby, everyone shall be saved.

3. Notice the future-pointing (Eschaton in the future) of this verse. And furthermore, John 17:3 says that a human *knowing* Jesus means that human is *saved*:

> And this is life eternal, that they might *know* thee the only true God, and Jesus Christ, whom thou hast sent. (John 17:3)

Hyper-Calvinist Universal Salvation

And *all* flesh *shall* see the salvation of God.[4] (Luke 3:6)

Multiple sections below are devoted to citing and analyzing Scripture that demonstrates the specific Eschaton-pointing metaphysics of Hyper-Calvinist universal salvation.

Notice the future-pointing nature of those three verses, where the word "shall" in each indicates that the universal salvation is positioned *in the future* of those verses, which is temporally located at the Eschaton. This future-pointing of verses to a future universalist Eschaton is a dominant theme of the copious Scripture cited in this book in support of Hyper-Calvinist universal salvation. There are even verses that are very widely discussed, such as "every knee shall bow," that describe the theology of Hyper-Calvinist universal salvation, as do these widely discussed verses:

> And I, if I be lifted up from the earth, *will draw all men* unto me. (John 12:32)

> Let *every thing* that hath breath praise the LORD. Praise ye the LORD.[5] (Ps 150:6)

And since Isa 49:26 indicates that *all* flesh shall *know*, then John 17:3 tells us that *all* will be saved.

4. Notice, again, the future-pointing of this verse. Some may claim that this verse is only referring to the future ministry of Jesus, not the Eschaton. But Luke 3:6 must refer to both, since the context of this verse is the Eschaton, as seen in the verse before, Luke 3:5 AKJV: "Every valley shall be filled, and every mountain and hill shall be brought low; and the crooked shall be made straight, and the rough ways shall be made smooth." All mountains being made low is a destruction of, or vanishing of, every mountain. This is a concept only found in Scripture to do with the Eschaton (see Rev 6:14 and 16:20; Ezek 38:20; and Ps 46:2–3, where Psalm 46 can be interpreted, at least in part, as a passage about the Eschaton, since it refers the end of wars in verse 7, and to the earth melting in verse 6). And more importantly, Luke 3:6 refers to all men *seeing* the salvation of GOD. *All* men seeing this is only an Eschaton event, since before the Eschaton, all men do not see Jesus/salvation. Luke 3:5–6 is repeated in Isa 40:4–5, but where is it is stated that the glory of the LORD shall be *revealed* to all flesh, which is an Eschaton scenario (see discussion below about 2 Thess 1:7–9), and where instead of all men seeing the salvation of the LORD, it is *all flesh* that see it together.

5. Above I just discussed the future-pointing of Scripture to a future universalism via the Lake of Fire (GOD), so does that mean that only in the future is this all-praise of the LORD established? Or are there ways in which that future event is being already felt, or lived? Discussion below will support that both are occurring (as John 12:32, just cited, also supports), and therefore, in addition to future-pointing Scripture that points to a future universalist Fire-Eschaton at the end of all things (1 Pet 4:7), we can *also* expect to find Scripture indicating that this future Eschaton-by-Fire is felt and experienced in some way *in the present*, as if the Eschaton was acting like a great attractor (to borrow a

Scriptural Support for Hyper-Calvinist Universal Salvation, Part 1

And a verse like Romans 5:6, also widely discussed, seemingly fits better into the Hyper-Calvinist universal salvation scenario than the popular view of hell:

> For when we were yet without strength, in due time Christ died for the ungodly.[6] (Rom 5:6)

---

term from astrophysics) from the future, invading into human souls and into all things, at the present. I say this because we know that the crucified GOD is, *now*, since his Ascension, *drawing all people to Him* (John 12:32), where we will all see Him as he really is for the first time in the early phases of the Eschaton (Isa 40:5; 1 John 3:2, more verse support given below). These verses (also include Acts 3:21) appear to establish that GOD is *presently drawing, pulling,* all people and all things, across time, *to* his future Eschaton revealing—such as if all humans now sense, and could now *feel*, be aware of, and interact with, this future event (in part), this Fire of the future in all of their present moments—as if his presence in our lives *now* contains a kindling or spark or smoldering about that power of the Fire-Eschaton. This is when humans first see him face-to-face (1 John 3:2), and as if that understanding of who he is as unveiled in the future is impacting people and all things *presently*:

> For the earnest expectation of the creature waiteth for the manifestation of the sons of God. (Rom 8:19)

So, it may be more accurate to suggest that all of creation has always "felt," for lack of better words, the pull of the Consuming Fire of the Eschaton. I believe that Psalm 150:6 could be interpreted as future pointing, due to the word "Let," which seems to be expressing that not all creatures that have breath are praising, so therefore, the LORD had to make the command, via Psalm 150, to let them do so at some point at or after his commanding. I wanted to bring up the idea that we can expect present-oriented verses about all creatures praising to be found in Scripture, about all creatures presently yearning for GOD and/or praising Him. It appears that John 1:9; Titus 2:11; and Mark 1:37 (KJV only for Mark 1:37) seem to be powerful examples of such universalist verses.

6. As a side point, it is interesting to note that since (1) Christ died for the ungodly (Rom 5:6)—which initially would be all people, both the elect and the condemned/unchosen, since *all* have fallen short of the glory of GOD—and since (2) Christ's death and resurrection led to the forgiveness of *all* sins (1 John 2:2; also see Mark 3:28 in KJV wording), then according to the popular view of hell, there would be multitudes of people in hell who *are forgiven* but nevertheless tortured in hell forever. This is a surprising form of "forgiveness," where the soul is forgiven, but regardless, the most horrific hell punishment is still carried out *forever*. This would be another one of the scriptural paradoxes cleared up with Hyper-Calvinist universal salvation.

5

Pre-Eschaton Annihilation

I WILL NEXT INTRODUCE *pre-Eschaton* annihilation theology, and describe how it is an element of Scripture, and of Hyper-Calvinist universal salvation. Those familiar with medieval mysticism might believe I could be referring to something like Margarette Poerete's ecstatic annihilation theology. While possibly related and containing some overlap with the pre-Eschaton annihilation I will introduce in this chapter, I will be discussing a scriptural model of pre-Eschaton annihilation that is not identical to Poerete's. To my knowledge, theologies of annihilation have been discussed by theologians sparsely over the past few hundred years, where they have been discussed as being alternative theories to the popular and traditional view of hell and God torturing in hell. Instead of one being put in hell torture forever, one is obliterated from existence forever. Such a view would be a *final* annihilation, never to be reversed, *after* the Eschaton: a post-Eschaton annihilation, not a pre-Eschaton annihilation. But in this book I point out that *pre-*Eschaton annihilation is the annihilation theology that is found in Scripture.

By pre-Eschaton annihilation, I am referring to a self-nonexistence for some souls, *from* the point of death of the physical body, *to* the resurrection at the start of the Eschaton. So, the self-nonexistence described in Scripture is not an *everlasting* annihilation *after* the Eschaton, as in standard annihilation theology, but rather, Scripture is describing a temporary self-nonexistence between physical body death and the Eschaton. And as for pre-Eschaton annihilation, there can be multiple pre-Eschaton annihilations for a person, and they are of two types: (1) annihilation before physical body death, and (2) annihilation after physical body death (but pre-Eschaton). There are differences between the two, and I will mainly be

Pre-Eschaton Annihilation

concerned with 2, the long dreamless sleep and unconsciousness (nonexistence of consciousness and of self) from the point of body death until the person is awakened by the LORD at the start of the Eschaton with the first resurrection (John 5:25–28).

In traditional annihilationist theology (post-Eschaton final annihilation), there is an end in time to the soul being an entity that exists in reality. In the traditional post-Eschaton final annihilation, theologians are not referring to a dormant soul, which still exists but just does not contain any content (mental content) in it, like a blank mind that does not have any thoughts or feelings in it. Rather, there is not even a dormant or blank mind or soul, ever again, from the point of the post-Eschaton annihilation nonexistence. But we can identify how this is *not* what Scripture is referring to in the annihilation verses—verses about souls ceasing to exist (being destroyed, for example). For example, look at this passage:

> 11 When thou with rebukes dost correct man for iniquity, thou makest his beauty to consume away like a moth: surely every man is vanity. Selah. 12 Hear my prayer, O LORD, and give ear unto my cry; hold not thy peace at my tears: for I am a stranger with thee, and a sojourner, as all my fathers were. 13 O spare me, that I may recover strength, before I go hence, *and be no more*. (Ps 39:11–13)

The verse is written as if the person is "no more" (ceasing to exist) at the end of his life, and thus at the point in time of body death, not at the Eschaton. This is not in agreement with traditional annihilationist theology (such as of the contemporary theologian Chris Date), which, to my knowledge, maintains that annihilation is initiated around the time of the Lake of Fire, after the second phase of the first resurrection (resurrection of the condemned, see Rev 20:5). Also, if the annihilation referred to in Psalm 39 were the final and permanent annihilation of the traditional post-Eschaton annihilation theology, then we would come to a fatal problem for the consistency of the Bible, since there is the first *resurrection* of John 5:25–29, Revelation 20:4–6, and so on, where the soon-to-be forever annihilated would be resurrected (*contradiction*).

So, something else must be going on. If we merely take Scripture for what it is saying, then we see two issues from what was just discussed about Psalm 39:11–13 and the Eschaton resurrection:

I. The person ceases to exist around the point of body-death (pre-Eschaton).

Hyper-Calvinist Universal Salvation

II. The person is brought back into existence (resurrected) at the Eschaton.

So, what would prevent us from merely, simply believing that both I and II are correct, as plainly stated in Scripture? Nothing that I can see, so I will follow Scripture in order to discover what it is saying—and it is saying, here, that the annihilation of the self (define self as the stream of consciousness) discussed in Scripture is (I) *pre-Eschaton*, and (II) temporary (temporally finite), like a *gap* in the existence of self. From what has just been written, the correct view of annihilation would be where annihilation is *finished* by the start of the Eschaton, and the incorrect view (traditional post-Eschaton annihilation theology) is where annihilation has *not yet started* at the start of the Eschaton.

The following is a description of the pre-Eschaton annihilationism and self-nonexistence that I will be extracting form Scripture. The soul exists in physical reality (pre-Eschaton) either as saved or condemned, and regardless of which state it is in at the time of physical death, the soul, for most humans, will be annihilated temporarily, meaning that it will not have any mental and self contents for a finite duration, specifically from the time of physical body death and up to when the LORD wakes the person from the grave at the Eschaton (John 5:25–28). Annihilation can also be thought of like a dreamless sleep and a sleep of death (see Ps 13:3), or a mind without any mental activity (without any thoughts or feelings), which is a state of nonexistence of self, since a self cannot exist without experiencing.[1] So, mental activity, mind, self, is annihilated, stopped, ended, and the soul is depicted in Scripture in a state of blankness, dormancy, nonactivity, and death. The annihilated soul is in death-sleep, without form or content. But this self-nonexistence is not unending, as with the aforementioned traditional model of post-Eschaton annihilationism, and instead, this state of annihilation and self-nonexistence *ends*—or rather, the self is brought back into existence, where the soul again has contents (it again has thoughts and feelings implanted into it by GOD; see Luke 11:39–40), at the start of the Eschaton, and by that the soul is brought back to life at the resurrection, back from annihilation-death, where soon after this time (soon after the time where annihilation was reversed), the soul will be made salvific,[2] by

---

1. Recall the first line of the Introduction of Immanual Kant's *Critique of Pure Reason*, which refers to all knowledge beginning with *experience*.

2. Here and throughout, I sometimes use this term *salvific* to refer to or describe the objects of salvation, as well as to describe what accomplishes or mediates salvation.

Pre-Eschaton Annihilation

seeing GOD as he truly is (at the Descension), and by being burned by GOD's Fire (Lake of Fire). That is what seems to be the model of reality seen in Scripture. All of these points will be unpacked below, backed with Scripture

Consider:

> 1 O LORD God of my salvation, I have cried day and night before thee: 2 let my prayer come before thee: incline thine ear unto my cry; 3 for my soul is full of troubles: and my life draweth nigh unto the grave. 4 I am counted with them that go down into the pit: I am as a man that hath no strength: 5 free among the dead, like the slain that lie in the grave, whom thou rememberest no more: and they are cut off from thy hand. 6 Thou hast laid me in the lowest pit, in darkness, in the deeps. 7 Thy wrath lieth hard upon me, and thou hast afflicted me with all thy waves. Selah. (Ps 88:1–7)

This passage involves some of the repeating themes about pre-Eschaton annihilation: being full of weakness and trouble at the annihilation, being laid in the darkness of the pit for sleep and/or death (annihilation, being "no more"), being forgotten by GOD, and where it is as if one is under the ocean (the waves of verse 7). We will see these themes repeat in other passages, and especially in Jonah 2, a very important annihilation passage, discussed below. Jonah being consumed by the sea beast is the first type of annihilation event: annihilation that occurs and is reversed all before death of the physical body. But what I will refer to as "annihilation" hereafter is the second type: self-nonexistence from the point of physical body death, up to and reversing at the Eschaton.

Annihilation brings a termination to the life of trouble (as seen in Psalm 88), and it brings one *directly* to the Eschaton resurrection. Pre-Eschaton annihilation involves the view that those who descend into the annihilated self-nonexistence at their body death will, experientially speaking, go *directly* to the Eschaton (first resurrection). The time of self-nonexistence involves the death of the body, on the one hand, and the Eschaton resurrection, on the other, abutting one another *directly* in time (in *experiential* time, that is, since there is no little or no experiencing during the annihilation). This seems to be roughly like when I was a child and I would believe that the moment I fell asleep, the morning would be there. And this would seem to be why some can see into the Eschaton and into their

---

GOD alone has full authority and sovereignty, and salvation is always the will and work of him alone.

Hyper-Calvinist Universal Salvation

afterlife salvation at the point of physical body death, and as they are going into the annihilation sleep/death, such as with the martyrdom of Stephen (Acts 6–7), where Stephen sees GOD and Jesus directly when he sees into heaven (Acts 7:56) as he is going to sleep at body death (Acts 7:60).

The following passage reflects what we see in the annihilationist verses: that a self is annihilated, brought into nonexistence, at a point associated with physical body death, and then brought back to life, resurrected/raised, at the end of the world (the Eschaton), as can be seen in this passage:

> 17 Like as a woman with child, that draweth near the time of her delivery, is in pain, and crieth out in her pangs; so have we been in thy sight, O LORD. 18 We have been with child, we have been in pain, we have as it were brought forth wind; we have not wrought any deliverance in the earth; neither have the inhabitants of the world fallen. 19 Thy dead men shall live, together with my dead body shall they arise. Awake and sing, ye that dwell in dust: for thy dew is as the dew of herbs, and the earth shall cast out the dead. 20 Come, my people, enter thou into thy chambers, and shut thy doors about thee: hide thyself as it were for a little moment, until the indignation be overpast. (Isa 26:17–20)

In considering the two passages we just looked at, Isaiah 26:17–20 and Psalm 39:11–13, Scripture indicates that there is a soul annihilation-sleep and self-nonexistence up to the Eschaton, wherein the selves that were nonexistent are brought back into existence at the Eschaton and for eternity. The nonexistence is a *sleep*, we know from Scripture, since, to give one example, we see in Jonah 2:7 that Jonah goes into the underworld, where he *sleeps* (faints, becomes unconscious, pause in conscious awareness), and when he awakens (begins his emergence from and out of the underworld) he is aware of the LORD. In Psalm 39:11–13, through David, GOD is telling humanity about how a human will feel the distance they have between their self and GOD before the Eschaton (*distance*, here, seemingly meaning that we do not see him directly yet, and only see him through a glass darkly, at this point, whereas at the Eschaton descending of GOD to the clouds we will see him as he is; see 1 Cor 13:12; 1 John 3:2). And before that, the human will go from the troubled state of physical existence (corrupted existence) into annihilation and self-nonexistence ("be no more").

In Psalm 88, we are told that the person is *free* in the annihilation-sleep nonexistence, indicating a positivity about the annihilation—contrary to how the psalm is usually described, as being quite gloomy and/or negative.

Pre-Eschaton Annihilation

In annihilation-sleep nonexistence, pain ceases to hurt, and one cannot sin, thus a person (that is, the dormant soul, the nonexistent self) is free in a way that the pre-annihilation person cannot be. Whereas the soul goes dormant (nonexistence of the self), the conscious experience of the person ceases to exist, and for that reason the consciousness will go directly from this life in physical reality to the next, which is the resurrection at the Eschaton, from physical embodied existence, experientially, as mentioned above. So, the time of annihilation, which is between physical bodily existence and the Eschaton, can be referred to as a time of nonexistence of the self, of the person, of the qualia, of the self-haecceity, which is how I will regard the annihilation phase, pre-Eschaton, for reasons seen in Psalm 39:11–13, but also due to passages like the following, which mentions that at death the unsaved man has his conscious contents (thoughts) cease to exist:

> 1 Praise ye the LORD. Praise the LORD, O my soul. 2 While I live will I praise the LORD: I will sing praises unto my God while I have any being. 3 Put not your trust in princes, nor in the son of man, in whom there is no help. 4 His breath goeth forth, he returneth to his earth; *in that very day his thoughts perish.* (Ps 146:1–4)

I work from the thesis in this book that if there are no contents of consciousness, then the self does not exist. Perhaps there is an empty container, the soul, that normally holds the contents of consciousness, that holds the self, that remains through pre-Eschaton annihilation, non-experiencing.[3]

---

3. Notice that I am referring to the self as the contents of consciousness that are imbued with qualia, and I am referring to self as if it exists in a container called the *soul*, wherein the soul can be emptied, as the self ceases to exist when vanishing into annihilation. That is how I am using these terms—"self," "soul," "qualia"—but one need not use them, and one can use whatever words they prefer. The point is that there is a situation where the person has an active part of their consciousness (which appears to be all we know of our selves, and thus this active part *is our selves*), and some of its primary contents are: linguistic sound-thought, intensities of feeling, inner visualizations, qualia, among other aspects of inner-subjective consciousness (which I call *the self*, but one can call it whatever they'd prefer), and where this active mind (self) may exist in a container or spiritual container of some sort, which I called *the soul*, but one can call it by whatever name one wants. And that is, *if* there is such a container that holds the self/mind contents—perhaps analogous to how stars are theorized to exist in, and be "held by," an unseen metaphysical and pre-scientific container, called *space*. We would have no scientific or experiential evidence for the existence of a container holding mind contents; it is a theoretical-logical entity deduced to exist: a place for self (mind contents) to exist so it is located *somewhere*, rather than *nowhere*, since it may not make sense to consider mind contents as existing in space-time (if space-time is a real, mind-independent entity).

Hyper-Calvinist Universal Salvation

Another reason I hold that the biggest annihilation, from the point of physical body death to the Eschaton, involves a scenario where one's consciousness and/or soul *ceases to exist*, is because there are places in Scripture where the soul is described as being *destroyed*, or being in eternal destruction. Consider the words of Jesus in the following verse:

> And fear not them which kill the body, but are not able to kill the soul: but rather fear him which is able to *destroy* both *soul* and body *in hell*. (Matt 10:28)[4]

This verse appears to indicate that what *hell* (which is only pre-Eschaton, as outlined in other chapters) actually *is*, or involves, is the *nonexistence of* (destruction of) *the self*: GOD bringing the self into nonexistence after body death. Now add to this how hell and the underworld regions are also destroyed at the Eschaton (Rev 20:14), when the earth—which the underworld regions are inside of—passes away (Matt 24:35; Mark 13:31; Luke 21:33; 2 Pet 3:10; Rev 21:1) at the end of all things (1 Pet 4:7), so the hell annihilation can only be *pre-Eschaton*. In Matthew 10:28, the modern translations are in accord with the KJV in using the word "destroy" ("kill" is also used), and in using the word "hell." Importantly, notice how this destruction (annihilation) happens specifically at the hell phase, which is pre-Eschaton, since hell is destroyed at the Eschaton (as pointed out above, and where entire sections below will verify this). This is a marked difference between mainstream *post-Eschaton* annihilation theology and the *pre-Eschaton* annihilation theology of this book. But the scriptural evidence is clear: it is *in hell* (pre-Eschaton) that annihilation occurs, not at the Eschaton and/or final judgment.

Consider the following additional examples of annihilation verses, specifically pointing to a *pre-Eschaton* annihilation of humans, that is temporary, ending at the Eschaton.

---

4. This verse mentions the idea of soul destruction, not just destruction of conscious contents (self, and self-experiencing). I have so far discussed mainly a scenario where the self is annihilated pre-Eschaton, where soul might remain and be dormant, but the position of this book is that the soul also could be destroyed, which Matt 10:28 says "is able" to happen, and that pre-Eschaton annihilation could very well involve both destruction of conscious experiencing (self) as well as destruction of the soul (the container of self). Perhaps different variations of these processes are applied to people differentially, as different mechanics are needed in the death (annihilation) and Eschaton resurrection processes GOD uses to save all people at the Eschaton.

Pre-Eschaton Annihilation

> For this we say unto you by the word of the Lord, that we which are alive and remain unto the coming of the Lord shall not prevent them which *are asleep*. (1 Thess 4:15)

> And the destruction of the transgressors and of the sinners shall be together, and they that forsake the LORD *shall be consumed*.[5] (Isa 1:28)

More verses about pre-Eschaton annihilation are cited below. And the following verses are about annihilation as everlasting destruction:

> Who shall be punished with everlasting *destruction* from the presence of the Lord, and from the glory of his power.[6] (2 Thess 1:9)

> When the wicked spring as the grass, and when all the workers of iniquity do flourish; it is that they *shall be destroyed for ever*. (Ps 92:7)

In a chapter below, I will discuss why Psalm 92:7, and others verses, such as Jonah 2:6, involve the concept of everlastingness, annihilation being a *forever* destruction, when all annihilated souls are brought back to life (resurrected). Note that Psalm 92:7 appears to indicate a pre-Eschaton annihilation, since they are destroyed (brought to nonexistence) as they are flourishing, before the resurrection of the condemned. So, the picture is as follows: the annihilated will be destroyed forever but also brought back into existence at the Eschaton, despite their being destroyed forever; GOD interrupts their everlasting state of annihilation when bringing them back into existence. As mentioned, this seeming discrepancy—destroyed forever, but not actually forever—will be explained in a chapter below.

Consider the following additional verses about the pre-Eschaton nonexistence/annihilation of self and soul, which also point to the resurrection of the soul, the soul coming out of death, and the self coming back into existence, from its *temporary* nonexistence (like a gap in time).

> Marvel not at this: for the hour is coming, in the which all that are in the graves shall hear[7] his voice, and shall come forth; they that

---

5. The concept here of the annihilated later being *consumed* will play an extremely important role in our development of Hyper-Calvinist universal salvation in this book.

6. I will discuss the relationship between eternal destruction (annihilation) and eternal punishment in a chapter below. Also, I will point out why temporary pre-Eschaton annihilation is described in some places in Scripture as everlasting, eternal, or forever, in a chapter below.

7. Some may wonder how the annihilated can *hear*. In this book, I hold the position

have done good, unto the resurrection of life; and they that have done evil, unto the resurrection of damnation. (John 5:28–29)

And the sea gave up the dead which were in it; and death and hell[8] delivered up the dead which were in them: and they were judged every man according to their works. (Rev 20:13)

---

that annihilation is primarily like some sort of dreamless sleep, perhaps, or a cessation of consciousness and conscious awareness, in some way. Some Scripture implies there is still a body of some sort during underworldly sleep-annihilation, and perhaps even an altered and/or spiritual-like body (see 1 Samuel 28), while other Scripture implies that the body would be destroyed (not exist) during underworldly annihilation/loss of consciousness (see Matt 10:28). For that reason, there may be an array of scenarios for underworldly body existence or nonexistence—where some have a body of some sort, and some do not. But this is all not what I am concerned with here. Rather, I am concerned with aspect of annihilation involving loss of conscious and the loss of consciousness as being the annihilation state: without consciousness and conscious awareness, the person—that is, the *self*—does not exist, and whether the body continues existing, *or* if the body is *also* destroyed (stops existing), would depend on the specific situation. A stoppage in consciousness and in conscious awareness can occur for a consciousness with a body, and for a consciousness that does not have a body (such as with the disembodied consciousness of the man Paul knew in 2 Cor 12:1–4). In either case, what appears to be going on is that the soul is dormant (by which I mean it does not have any conscious activity, it is devoid of conscious contents, as discussed above), and the LORD begins its awakening when he calls to it at the Eschaton, whereby the hearing happens in consciousness, not via the ears of a body. This seems to align well with what we humans recognize as *hearing*, since all hearing happens in consciousness—ears seemingly are merely a detector of air vibrations to be processed "downstream" in brain and mind, wherein the diverse phenomenology of sound experiences is an aspect of consciousness, more than of ear drums. And this seems to align with the concept that the soul (regardless if it has a body or not) appears to stay in existence in the underworld, like a soul without consciousness and conscious awareness (the aforementioned dormant soul), but where the person, the self (the conscious elements and conscious awareness) do not exist (1 Samuel 28 seems to implies this): the dormant soul is a fully empty soul (fully empty of consciousness). The hearing of the LORD would be the LORD implanting the dormant soul with consciousness (see Luke 11:39–40) again at the Eschaton awakening. But the scenario where not even the dormant/empty soul exists also seems logical and possible, where in that scenario, the LORD could stop the existence of every aspect of a person, body, soul, consciousness, only to bring them back into existence—bringing back their body, their haecceity, subjective mind, qualia, etc., as he chooses—at the Eschaton awakening/resurrection. Perhaps, as the Scripture passages cited in this footnote imply, both scenarios (keeping dormant soul in existence, and not keeping it in existence) are what GOD is doing, depending on his predestining of the specific person (soul and living soul) in question, and their destiny that the LORD has determined before the beginning (see Grupp, "Why God Did Not Choose All Souls," for more discussion of this topic).

8. The use of the specific word "hell" here will be analyzed in detail later in this book. This is the only reference to people being "in hell" that I am are of in the King James Bible. There is no mention of people burning, and the Greek word is *hades*, which is not

Pre-Eschaton Annihilation

5 to deliver such an one unto Satan for the destruction of the flesh, that the spirit may be saved in the day of the Lord Jesus. 6 Your glorying is not good. Know ye not that a little leaven leaveneth the whole lump? (1 Cor 5:5–6)

And many of them that sleep[9] in the dust of the earth *shall awake*, some to everlasting life, and some to shame and everlasting contempt.[10] (Dan 12:2)

And have hope toward God, which they themselves also allow, that there shall be a resurrection of the dead, both of the just and unjust. (Acts 24:15)

25 For when they shall rise from the dead, they neither marry, nor are given in marriage; but are as the angels which are in heaven. 26 And as touching the dead, that they rise: have ye not read in the book of Moses, how in the bush God spake unto him, saying, I am the God of Abraham, and the God of Isaac, and the God of Jacob? 27 He is not the God of the dead, but the God of the living: ye therefore do greatly err. (Mark 12:25–27)

20 But now is Christ risen from the dead, and become the firstfruits of them that slept. 21 For since by man came death, by man came also the resurrection of the dead. 22 For as in Adam all die, even so in Christ shall all be made alive. (1 Cor 15:20–22)

Thy dead men shall live, together with my dead body shall they arise. Awake and sing, ye that dwell in dust: for thy dew is as the dew of herbs, and the earth shall cast out the dead. (Isa 26:19)

. . . and said unto them, Thus it is written, and thus it behoved Christ to suffer, and to rise from the dead the third day . . .[11] (Luke 24:46)

The verses just cited, as with others above, indicate that the annihilation is pre-Eschaton, and the resurrection of all people is *at* the Eschaton, revealing annihilation nonexistence to be temporary. And there is no scriptural evidence that the annihilation of the soul *starts*— rather than *ends*,

---

a place of fire, but of sleep.

9. Sleep here is a reference to the underworld existence in annihilation, seen also in some of the aforementioned verses in this chapter about annihilation nonexistence. Compare the fainting (loss of consciousness, sleep) of Jonah in the deep in Jonah 2.

10. I will discuss "everlasting contempt" in a chapter below.

11. All humans are in the image of Christ, and since GOD (Christ) has overcome death, we who are in his image also overcome death.

as I am pointing out—at a final judgement and with the Eschaton. These verses involve humans being awakened, resurrected, coming out of the land of the dead, for the Eschaton. They are emerging from either cessation of consciousness and/or soul annihilation of the underworld phase. The annihilation is *from* the point of body death *to* the Eschaton.

The annihilation of the soul is a *gap*, of some sort, in total destruction of the soul into dormancy, and thus a temporary nonexistence of the self. This is important because, in this book, I do not take a position on whether the soul (in addition to the self) ceases via sleep during contentless dormancy (annihilation) for a bit, on the one hand, or, on the other, if the soul literally stops existing, it is blotted out of existence, at the pre-Eschaton annihilation. Both sorts of annihilation may be occurring. And there appears to be a spectrum, a range, of ways the annihilation could occur, from mere sleep (dormant soul and nonexistent mind) to total nonexistence of the human even to the point of the soul ceasing to exist. But in this book, I am primarily concerned with annihilation as a cessation of consciousness and conscious awareness (self-nonexistence), which constitutes an end of the person, *from* the point of physical body death, *to* the Eschaton resurrection—a pause, silence, gap, sleep of conscious existence, of conscious awareness—wherein the self ceases to exist for a finite duration (but which is an eternity to the annihilated, discussed below) during the underworld interval.

This book involves the concept that all people, all selves, if re-created in a wink for the eternity with GOD in the afterlife, have to cease existing so that a *new* person, the new self, the new soul, of the afterlife can be created by the LORD. The old must vanish so the new can come into existence (2 Cor 5:17), wherein there will be a gap of annihilation/nonexistence between the two lives. If there were not a *gap* of annihilation/nonexistence, a separation between the two lives, the salvific and nonsalvific selves, would connect, interact, mingle, and since they are ultimately each the same self (the same haecceity): they would be identical at the point of connection-interaction of the two selves in the flow of time, just as two entities that touch must ultimately occupy the same location at their touching/interacting borders, lest they not be touching or interacting. The existence of the *corrupted* soul ceases, but then at a later time the *noncorrupted* living soul comes into existence:

> So also is the resurrection of the dead. It is sown in corruption; it is raised in incorruption... (1 Cor 15:42)

Pre-Eschaton Annihilation

A discontinuity, a gap, in the life of the self, and possibly the soul, occurs between these two existences (between life in the physical dimension in a physical body and the new angel body [Luke 20:36 KJV wording] obtained at the Eschaton), despite the body and its soul having its haecceity in both lives (the haecceity is brought back into existence after the gap, the annihilation interval[12]). If haecceity is lost, then GOD will resurrect it at the Eschaton. This haecceity gap is the annihilation interval of the living soul, where in the gap it is the dead soul, where consciousness and/or the soul ceases to function, and/or ceases to exist, during its time in the underworld. The loss of conscious functioning would be a cessation of mentation, wherein the self, experientially, would be described as no longer existing (annihilation). Since the soul is described as "dead" in Scripture, it would seem that the view that the soul stays in a death state in the underworld between physical body life and the Eschaton resurrection, having some sort of dormant existence, rather than being truly nonexistent during this interval gap, is the correct view.

If Scripture involves, at the very least, an annihilation of the person that consists of the annihilation *of consciousness*, this would therefore entail that a person is held to be, to some large degree, identical to their consciousness: if I don't have consciousness and conscious awareness, my self, my being, is paused and/or nonexistent during that interval. If consciousness ceases in some such way, then the person stops existing, in full or in part. A verse such as 1 Samuel 16:7 would indicate that our real self, the one GOD looks at and is looking at now, is our subjective, conscious, self-aware, inner landscape, and *not* primarily our bodies. John 6:63 says that "It is the spirit that quickeneth; the flesh profiteth nothing." The spirit is the consciousness primarily, more than the flesh.

To verify this position—that a human being is to be primarily defined in terms of its inner consciousness, rather than its physical body—in

---

12. There is a tremendous amount of discussion about the continuity of a person, especially in philosophical journals. In this book, I not only do not put any importance on the continuity of a person from the time of their first moments and on into the afterlife, but I claim that the Bible is denying such exists (for example, see the verse cited above, Ps 88:5). My claim, as just written, is that GOD, who is all-powerful, can make the qualia and the haecceity of the person cease to exist, and then bring it back into existence, as often as he wishes (see Ps 115:3), where he merely has to apply the same haecceity and qualia, and/or whatever else is needed, so that the very same self comes back into existence, just as they were before, by GOD's power, despite being discontinuous. Discontinuity of the person is largely what many of the debates in contemporary philosophy are about (such as the endurantism versus perdurantism debate).

philosophical terms, consider that if my consciousness could be removed from association with, or attachment to, my body, and/or from being inside of my physical fleshly body, and put into another container (body, instrument, vessel), such as some sort of a computer, for the sake of explanation, then hypothetically speaking, I believe I would still feel like, and have self-awareness of, my same conscious self—only moved to a different location and vessel, now inside of, or associated with, a new body (the computer). Phenomenologically, if I have anything like a normal consciousness after this shift has been made, I will still feel that I am "Jeff," and the very *same* "Jeff," regardless of which body my mind/consciousness is in—just as I feel the same continuity of selfhood (feeling I am the same "me," the same "I") when I am in a different body during a dream at night, where I dream I am in a different life, in a different world, with a different body. But if, in an inverse scenario, my body were preserved but not my mind, destroying my mind, my consciousness, even my soul, I would not feel I continue to exist, and my *self* would cease to exist, in some way.

This seems to support how the self is to a large degree, if not fully, identical to consciousness and/or conscious awareness. And for these reasons, I am taking the view of self as being more aligned with being consciousness and conscious awareness, rather than being the physical body, as logically inferred by what was just written in the previous paragraph. In different words, the self is the *inner awareness*, the inner *feeling* of self (including the qualia), the contents of consciousness, and all of the phenomenological self (in Husserlian terms), more than being the mere flesh-body with its meaty organs. So, if the inner self, the consciousness, ceases its activity, and there is no consciousness, then I conclude that the self does not exist in times of soul sleep (soul dormancy, without any conscious contents in it): the self is in a state of nonexistence. Without awareness, and without contents of consciousness, there is no self, or functioning self—only, at most, a dormant (nonactive) soul.

When the dead are raised at the Eschaton, at the coming-back-into-existence of the soul and/or the consciousness, from the underworld annihilation, the person is *brought back into existence* from this nonexistence and/or nonfunctioning of self and/or soul. Regardless of the exact nature of the annihilation happenings, and if there is some sort of spectrum, from sleep, on the one hand, to pure nonexistence (even to the point of the nonexistence of the dormant soul, which I argued against above), on the other, whatever its nature, we know that annihilation is reversed at the Eschaton, as just discussed. The references in Scripture about underworld existence being associated with a deep sleep (loss of consciousness) describe the time of annihilation and nonexistence, and the re-existence of the self:

> For as the body without the spirit is dead, so faith without works is dead also. (Jas 2:26)

> And the graves were opened; and many bodies of the saints which slept arose. (Matt 27:52)

> He said unto them, Give place: for the maid is not dead, but sleepeth. And they laughed him to scorn. (Matt 9:24)

> 54 When they heard these things, they were cut to the heart, and they gnashed on him with their teeth. 55 But he, being full of the Holy Ghost, looked up stedfastly into heaven, and saw the glory of God, and Jesus standing on the right hand of God, 56 and said, Behold, I see the heavens opened, and the Son of man standing on the right hand of God. 57 Then they cried out with a loud voice, and stopped their ears, and ran upon him with one accord, 58 and cast him out of the city, and stoned him: and the witnesses laid down their clothes at a young man's feet, whose name was Saul. 59 And they stoned Stephen, calling upon God, and saying, Lord Jesus, receive my spirit. 60 And he kneeled down, and cried with a loud voice, Lord, lay not this sin to their charge. And when he had said this, *he fell asleep*. (Acts 7:54–60)

> 50 But when Jesus heard it, he answered him, saying, Fear not: believe only, and she shall be made whole. 51 And when he came into the house, he suffered no man to go in, save Peter, and James, and John, and the father and the mother of the maiden. 52 And all wept, and bewailed her: but he said, Weep not; *she is not dead, but sleepeth*. 53 And they laughed him to scorn, knowing that she was dead. 54 And he put them all out, and took her by the hand, and called, saying, Maid, arise. 55 *And her spirit came again*, and she arose straightway: and he commanded to give her meat. (Luke 8:50–55)

> 11 These things said he: and after that he saith unto them, Our friend Lazarus sleepeth; but I go, that I may awake him out of sleep. 12 Then said his disciples, Lord, if he sleep, he shall do well. 13 Howbeit Jesus spake of his death: but they thought that he had spoken of taking of rest in sleep. 14 Then said Jesus unto them plainly, Lazarus is dead. (John 11:11–14)

Hyper-Calvinist Universal Salvation

> For the indignation of the Lord is upon all nations, and his fury upon all their armies: *he hath utterly destroyed them*, he hath delivered them to the slaughter. (Isa 34:2)

Traditional (pre-Eschaton) annihilationists typically hold, to my knowledge, that the soul ceases to exist at the final judgment, at the Eschaton, but the Hyper-Calvinist universal salvation theology described in this chapter would involve the idea that the Eschaton is the point where the self, and perhaps even the soul, in fact, *awakens*, by being brought back into existence, into awareness, back into consciousness, into having mental activity and mental content: *from* being in a state of unconsciousness, or perhaps of nonconsciousness. This is when the soul is *brought out of* the underworldly status. Consider the following verse:

> Because thou wilt not leave my soul in hell, neither wilt thou suffer thine Holy One to see corruption. (Acts 2:27)

6

The Two Stages of Salvation in Hyper-Calvinist Universal Salvation

NEXT, WE WILL FURTHER discuss the aforementioned two stages of salvation by the LORD, introduced above.

At first glance, the reader might believe that the concept of Hyper-Calvinist universal salvation would involve an impossible (contradictory) combination of ideas: *few*[1] are chosen (Matt 22:14), but *all* are saved—like claiming that all are saved and all are not saved, a blatant contradiction. But this only arises if GOD condemning people is fully *simultaneous with* him saving all people. That would amount to saying that GOD simultaneously saves *few* and saves *all* (contradiction). It is the *two-step* salvific process introduced above, where the two stages—first pre-Eschaton, and *after* that the all-saving Eschaton—are *not* simultaneous, that avoids any such contradiction. And this two-stage metaphysics is precisely what Scripture involves.

Verses in Scripture that refer to there being unsaved/condemned people are written about in parts of the Bible that are about a pre-Eschaton epoch, such as right now. And the vast majority of the universal salvation verses in the Bible not only talk about all being saved, but further, they refer to an omnisalvation of humanity in the future: at the end of the world. And then, on the other hand, verses that refer to events at the Eschaton move into only being about the salvific, as if there are no more unsaved/condemned people: where both the chosen and the condemned have been saved in the future.

---

1. See Grupp, "Why God Did Not Choose All Souls," for discussion for specifically *why* GOD only can choose *some*, not all, *before* the Eschaton.

Hyper-Calvinist Universal Salvation

> And this is the Father's will which hath sent me, that of *all* which he hath given me[2] I should lose nothing, *but should raise it up again at the last day.* (John 6:39)

The verses about the Eschaton (and/or post-Eschaton) are typically future-pointing, just as John 6:39 refers to all being raised not today, but in the future, on the last day (in the Eschaton events). Consider the following additional examples, where I have again italicized the future-pointing aspects, going *from* the present (pre-Eschaton) state, *to* being consumed by Fire at the Eschaton.

> And the vessel that he made of clay was marred in the hand of the potter: *so he made it again* another vessel, as seemed good to the potter to make it.[3] (Jer 18:4)

> Therefore judge nothing before the time, until the Lord come, who both *will bring* to light the hidden things of darkness, and *will make* manifest the counsels of the hearts: and *then* shall *every man have praise of God.* (1 Cor 4:5)

> 25 Verily, verily, I say unto you, The hour *is coming, and now is,*[4] when the dead *shall hear* the voice of the Son of God: and they that hear *shall live* . . . 28 Marvel not at this: for the hour *is coming*, in which all that are in the graves *shall hear* his voice, 29 and *shall come forth*; they that have done good, unto the resurrection of life;

---

2. And note that Jesus was given all things; see John 3:35 and 17:2; Matt 11:27 and 28:18.

3. This verse is another good example—as many given in this book are—of Scriptures that are about both historical events in the past and the universal salvation of the Eschaton. The same could be said of some of the verses I cite right after this one in this chapter and the next. As has been pointed out above, Scripture involves such fractal-like iterations and repetitions, such as with the days of Noah resembling the times leading into Eschaton, to give one of many examples that could have been given.

4. This phrase, "The hour is coming, and now is . . . ," a highly philosophical wording, indicates that the Eschaton has not come into being yet, but is both, for lack of better words, interacting with humans now, from the future, pulling humans to the Eschaton. But beyond that, and in another way, the Eschaton Fire is also *here*, now, where only part of it is unveiled to humans pre-Eschaton, where this partial awareness of GOD's presence (see 1 Cor 13:12) reveals GOD-Christ as the saving Fire, where at the Eschaton, when consumed while the world is burning (Lake of Fire), may be the very first time humans see GOD as he is, and therefore humans will be their real selves at that time (1 John 3:2). In that Presence (YHWH) now, in part, and in that Presence is our calling, which is to be salted with Fire (Mark 9:49).

The Two Stages of Salvation in Hyper-Calvinist Universal Salvation

> and they that have done evil, unto the resurrection of damnation.[5] (John 5:25, 28–29)

> Every man's work shall be made manifest: for the day *shall declare it*, because it *shall be* revealed by fire; and the fire *shall try* every man's work of what sort it is. (1 Cor 3:13)

One can see the aforementioned two-step salvific process in verses such as these. And from these Scriptures, which point to a future salvation of all unchosen souls by Eschaton Fire, the following two stages of salvation can be formulated, as follows:

> Two Stages of Salvation: (1) Scripture refers to there being both saved and unsaved souls *before* the Eschaton. Only the chosen are saved pre-Eschaton, and the unchosen are condemned during the pre-Eschaton stage. Pre-Eschaton, the chosen undergo an initial salvation and eternal seal[6] (Eph 4:30), saved by GOD's choosing (1 Pet 2:9; Deut 7:6), and by their being indwelt by him. But the unchosen are not made salvific pre-Eschaton (meaning they remain condemned up to the Eschaton). After this, (2) the unchosen are saved by the Lightning (Luke 17:24; 1 John 3:2) of GOD, and by the Descension of GOD at the Eschaton, to be refined and purified in the Lake of Fire (GOD) during the Eschaton event. At 1 only some are saved, until 2, where all remaining are saved: two steps or stages of salvation.

And consider these additional passages that indicate these two stages of salvation in Scripture:

> 15 For, behold, the LORD *will come with fire*, and with his chariots like a whirlwind, to render his anger with fury, and his rebuke *with flames of fire*. 16 For *by fire* and by his sword will the LORD plead with all flesh: and the slain of the LORD shall be many. 17 They that sanctify themselves, and purify themselves in the gardens behind one tree in the midst, eating swine's flesh, and the abomination, and the mouse, shall be consumed together, saith the LORD. (Isa 66:15–17)

This passage again links the Eschaton Fire with a baptism and purification (the Baptism of Fire).

---

5. Notice how verse 28 is not distinguishing between the righteous and unrighteous, and therefore even in and by unrighteousness the unsaved will be saved (see Romans 6).

6. The seal must be eternal since a chosen person cannot ever be not chosen. Therefore, chosen people, when sealed, can never be unsealed (eternal security).

Hyper-Calvinist Universal Salvation

The two-step salvific mechanics would likely have many dimensions of depth. For example, an event such as *the salvation of a soul* would have aspects to it not understandable by humans pre-Eschaton. I interpret the salvation of a soul to be where in some way the soul is coinhered, or made one with, its Creator, but which is a "process" of such depth and inexplicableness that our human language cannot grasp at this time (pre-Eschaton).[7] Similarly, we should expect that there are multiple dimensions, maybe even infinite dimensions, to any verse or passage of Scripture, to *every* aspect of Scripture, and therefore including the many verses and passages of Scripture that are specifically about Hyper-Calvinist universal salvation. So, while the formula of a two-step Hyper-Calvinist universal salvation appears in Scripture, the reader should *not* further conclude that there are *not* more, deeper dimensions about salvation to be contemplated and discovered. Consider the following passage:

> 7 and to you who are troubled rest with us, when the Lord Jesus shall be revealed from heaven with his mighty angels, 8 in flaming fire taking vengeance on them *that know not God*, and that *obey not* the gospel of our Lord Jesus Christ: 9 who *shall be punished with everlasting destruction from the presence of the Lord*, and from the glory of his power; 10 *when he shall come to be glorified in his saints*, and to be admired in all them that believe (because our testimony among you was believed) in that day. (2 Thess 1:7–10)

At first glance, it may appear that the italicized part, "punished with everlasting destruction from the presence of the Lord," is about the Eschaton Fire, since this text is sandwiched in between two parts of Scripture clearly about the Eschaton event. But the "know not" and "obey not" of verse 8, written in present tense, not past tense ("who did not obey"), indicates that in verse 8 the discussion is about humans who *are* disobedient, and therefore about a pre-Eschaton time, rather than a post-Eschaton time when there is no more disobedience. So, in 2 Thessalonians, the Writer[8] is talking about the present, while mentioning the future. Therefore, the eternal punishment with everlasting destruction from the presence of the LORD is pre-Eschaton, and thus referring to the underworldly existence of some

---

7. Rom 6:19–20 indicates how our human language and ways of understanding do not capture reality as it really is.

8. I am capitalizing the W, as a reference to GOD, to indicate the dictation view, rather than the inspiration view, of Scripture. To my knowledge, the dictation view was the view that Calvin also ascribed to (see Hesslink, "Revelation of God in Creation and Scripture," 7–8).

The Two Stages of Salvation in Hyper-Calvinist Universal Salvation

who have died in their bodies and still rest in the earth. And for these reasons, the annihilation discussed in the passage ("everlasting destruction") is another scriptural reference to the pre-Eschaton annihilation of the self between body death and the Eschaton for the unchosen.

Interestingly, the punishment and destruction (annihilation) of 2 Thessalonians is *from* the presence of the LORD. The word translated "from" is ἀπὸ, which is like "out of" (as used in Matt 12:43; 15:22; 24:27), and "because of" (as used in Matt 10:28; 18:7). So, it is *by the presence of GOD* that the soul, the mind, in the infinity of time cessation, pauses its functioning, sleeps in a contentless (no mental content) nonexistence. So, GOD's presence—his presence, *specifically*—is a catalyst of annihilation. The corrupted soul, the sin-filled soul, which cannot be saved *until* the Eschaton, but which *will be* at the Eschaton (see 1 Cor 5:5), appears to reside in the underworlds, sleeping dreamlessly (the aforementioned self-nonexistence) in a state of soul pause, or nonexistence of mental functioning, due to merely waiting for the Eschaton salvation.

7

Eternal Punishment

AND WHAT ABOUT EVERLASTING punishment? In Matthew 25, we see the soul annihilation of the underworld referred to as "everlasting punishment." In other words, I consider the "everlasting punishment" of Matthew 25 to be a synonym for everlasting destruction (self nonexistence): a person is destroyed for an infinity of time,[1] for specific reasons I will spell out in this chapter.

> And these shall go away *into* everlasting punishment: but the righteous into life eternal.[2] (Matt 25:46)

It must be the case that the "eternal punishment" referred to here is *equal to* eternal destruction (and therefore also equal to annihilation self-nonexistence), for if that were *not* the case, a contradiction would be located in Scripture, which is not possible. If eternal punishment was not *also* annihilation (eternal destruction), where the two were synonyms of each other, then one verse in Scripture—

---

1. To repeat, specifically what "everlasting" means in Matt 25:46 will be discussed in detail in a chapter below, where it will be explained how, in Scripture, annihilation is an infinity of temporal depth, rather than an infinity of temporal length (everlastingness).

2. This verse is about the Lake of Fire, not about hell. Hell is not temporally infinite, but the Lake of Fire is. This will be discussed below. This verse is about the goats, who appear to go into *everlasting* fire (Lake of Fire):

> Then shall he say also unto them on the left hand, Depart from me, ye cursed, into everlasting fire, prepared for the devil and his angels. (Matt 25:41)

The more modern translations say "eternal fire."

Eternal Punishment

> And fear not them which kill the body, but are not able to kill the soul: but rather fear him which is able to destroy both soul[3] and body in hell. (Matt 10:28)

—would involve a person *ceasing to exist* (via being destroyed) during annihilation punishment (the punishment of hell destruction/annihilation), and another verse (Matt 25:46, just cited above) would point to the opposite: punishment while being non-annihilated (not destroyed). Therefore, Matthew 25:46 would be in contradiction with Matthew 10:28, and the obvious way to avoid this contradiction is, as stated, if the eternal punishment of Matthew 25:46 is equal to annihilation of the soul and/or person.[4]

There is more support for this concept that eternal *destruction* is synonymous with eternal *punishment* if we consider the following passage:

> 7 And to you who are troubled rest with us, when the Lord Jesus shall be revealed from heaven with his mighty angels, 8 In flaming fire taking vengeance on them that know not God, and that obey not the gospel of our Lord Jesus Christ: 9 Who shall be punished with everlasting destruction from the presence of the Lord, and from the glory of his power; 10 When he shall come to be glorified in his saints, and to be admired in all them that believe (because our testimony among you was believed) in that day. (2 Thess 1:7–10)

1:9, a verse about annihilation (destruction) of an unchosen person, indicates that the destruction of the person is a *separation from* GOD's presence (ἀπό, from or *away* from). But there *cannot be* any such separation from GOD's presence, since one can never be away from the omnipresent GOD and the love of GOD:

> For I am persuaded, that neither death, nor life, nor angels, nor principalities, nor powers, nor things present, nor things to come, nor height, nor depth, nor any other creature, shall be able to separate us from the love of God, which is in Christ Jesus our Lord. (Rom 8:38–39)

> If I ascend up into heaven, thou art there: if I make my bed in hell,[5] behold, thou art there. (Ps 139:8)

---

3. Interestingly, the verse even indicates that even *the soul* blinks into nonexistence, at least in the case of this instance of annihilation referred to in Scripture.

4. This is also the position endorsed by Bart Ehrman (Ehrman, "Smith-Pettit Lecture," 38:56).

5. The newer translations use "Hades" rather than "hell."

Hyper-Calvinist Universal Salvation

Therefore, the *separation* from GOD's presence referred to in 2 Thessalonians 1:9 must be a reference to the pre-Eschaton annihilation: cessation and annihilation of, at the very least, their conscious awareness and their mind (self), if not also (at least for some) their soul. If there was no such annihilation, then the person would be both *separated from* GOD's presence and *also in* GOD's presence (since they are in his love [Rom 8:38–39], which is to be in his presence, since GOD is love [1 John 4:7–9]), which is a contradiction, since the person would be simultaneously separated and not separated (a textbook contradiction) from GOD. Annihilation of the self (regardless of whether that means soul sleep, on the one hand [self-nonexistence], or soul nonexistence, on the other), where the separation occurs because a person (human self) ceases to exist, and therein is not with GOD (is separated from him), resolves this, and there is no contradiction in Scripture. GOD is omnipresent and omnitemporal, so the only way a human self can be referred to as "separated" from GOD is for the self to *not exist*—wherein, indeed, in that scenario, GOD *is separated* from the self.

The logical findings of this chapter reveal the perfect logic of Scripture, which is little known to men whose minds have been blinded. I contend that Scripture contains a perfect logic; however, men do not see it, and instead attempt to describe it by their own reasoning and understanding—through their minds, which are smaller than the infinite Consciousness (YHWH, Θεός) that created them.

8

The Inevitable Gap of Annihilation Self-Nonexistence

BEFORE RETURNING TO ANALYSIS of Matthew 25:41, one more possible objection to the theology of pre-Eschaton annihilation should be discussed. The objection can be stated as follows: if one's consciousness (self), and possibly also their dormant soul, does not exist through the underworld gap from annihilation self-nonexistence at body death to the Eschaton, then why does Scripture refer to eternal or everlasting *punishment*, when the consciousness, and maybe even the soul, does not exist? *How can punishment be happening if there is nothing there to punish?* I will next address this objection.

There are no words we can use to describe the self, and possibly also the soul, during the gap of annihilation self-nonexistence, since the consciousness (self) does not exist. There is not anything that can be referred to, no entity of any sort to assign language to—there are no words we can say about a self and/or soul that *is not there*. There are merely two distinct lives, two separated existences, being one and the same haecceity existing at distinct spans of time, both during the pre-Eschaton, pre-underworld existence of the person, on the one hand, and the Eschaton/post-Eschaton existence of the person on the other. The point is that the pre-afterlife (pre-Eschaton, pre-underworld) existence of the consciousness (self) and/or the soul has to *stop existing*, and the afterlife (Eschaton/post-Eschaton) consciousness (self) and/or soul must *come into existence* after the annihilation nonexistence gap, as a *new entity*, but nevertheless the same haecceity.

These two existences cannot touch each other, so to speak. In other words, they cannot temporally coincide at their boundaries in any way.

For example: the end of the pre-Eschaton consciousness (self) and/or soul cannot temporally coincide in any way with the start of the Eschaton/post-Eschaton consciousness (self) and/or soul. If they did, then at the overlap/coinciding interval, the consciousness and/or soul would exist both simultaneously in the pre-Eschaton state, on the one hand, and also in the Eschaton and post-Eschaton state, on the other, during that duration of overlap of the two existences of the consciousness and/or soul. If that happened, then a person would be both able to see GOD as he is (1 John 3:2) and *not* able to see GOD as he is, which is a contradiction, and therefore not possible.

We will, however, find that if time is continuous, where the moments of the timeline are lined up like the Real number line (that is, the mathematical number line of all Real numbers, both rational and irrational numbers, which have the density of a plenum), in that scenario the pre- and post-Eschaton lives of a consciousness and/or self also cannot be directly adjacent if there is no overlap, and there must be an inevitable gap (annihilation). On this scenario, of continuous time, atoms of time (called chronons) are point-sized (having no duration, no temporal size), wherein any duration of time is composed of timeless/durationless instants (points of time), apparently infinities of them composing any perceived duration. Consider what philosopher Roderick Chisholm discusses, in how entities cannot touch at all, in any scenario of continuous time or space:

> Consider two discrete physical bodies thought to be continuous with each other; the east side of body A, say, is continuous with the west side of body B. How is this possible? Either (i) the eastmost part of A is in the same place as is the westmost part of B or (ii) no part of A occupies the same place as does any part of B. In the case of (i), we would have two discrete things in the same place. But this is impossible. In the case of (ii), since A and B occupy different places, there is a place between the place where A is and the place where B is. But if there is a place between A and B, then A and B are not continuous.[1]

Therefore, there can *only* be a temporal gap (nonexistence) *between* the two lives (pre-Eschaton and Eschaton/post-Eschaton consciousness/self, and possibly also the soul), which is the pre-Eschaton annihilation. The only logical and possible scenario is the aforementioned annihilation gap of self-nonexistence and absolute soul dormancy or nonexistence between

---

1. Chisholm, *On Metaphysics*, 84.

The Inevitable Gap of Annihilation Self-Nonexistence

the two lives, and a pre-Eschaton annihilation is logically inevitable. The pre-Eschaton self has to cease existing in order that a new self can come into existence. The old self that is capable of sin must end before the Eschaton and commencement of afterlife, where the afterlife self is created at the Eschaton resurrection. The afterlife self is new, but it has the same haecceity as previously existed, wherein the haecceity of the self must be new when resurrected, a newness, at the time as when GOD makes all things new (Rev 21:5). As Chisholm pointed out, there can only be a gap (annihilation) between these pre- and post-Eschaton self existences, so annihilation is inevitable, which is why Scripture is replete with this pre-Eschaton annihilation message:

> 1 Man that is born of a woman is of few days, and full of trouble. 2 He cometh forth like a flower, and is cut down: he fleeth also as a shadow, and continueth not. 3 And dost thou open thine eyes upon such an one, and bringest me into judgment with thee? 4 Who can bring a clean thing out of an unclean? not one… 5 Seeing his days are determined, the number of his months are with thee, thou hast appointed his bounds that he cannot pass… 7 For there is hope of a tree, if it be cut down, that it will sprout again, and that the tender branch thereof will not cease. 10 But man dieth, and wasteth away: yea, man giveth up the ghost, and where is he? 11 As the waters fail from the sea, and the flood decayeth and drieth up: 12 so man lieth down, and riseth not: till the heavens be no more, they shall not awake, nor be raised out of their sleep. 13 O that thou wouldest hide me in the grave, that thou wouldest keep me secret, until thy wrath be past, that thou wouldest appoint me a set time, and remember me! 14 If a man die, shall he live again? all the days of my appointed time will I wait, till my change come. 15 Thou shalt call, and I will answer thee: thou wilt have a desire to the work of thine hands. (Job 14: 1–4,5,7,10–15)

Further, this is more reason for why eternal punishment has to be identical to eternal destruction (annihilation), and whatever the nature of the punishment, it is tied, at least in part, to pre-Eschaton self-nonexistence.

We also know that the traditional theory of annihilationism (post-Eschaton), which the findings of this book are in disagreement with, cannot be correct, since *all* people are *to be* saved, as Scripture so precisely verifies. If *all* human souls are to be saved, then there cannot be souls that are annihilated *without end*, annihilated without being lifted up and resurrected. For if they were, then all would not be saved, and the plethora of

Hyper-Calvinist Universal Salvation

Scripture passages cited in this book verifying scriptural Hyper-Calvinist universal salvation would be contradicted: permanently annihilated (nonexistent) consciousnesses and/or souls would be saved (*contradiction*). And for that reason, the only annihilation that Scripture can be referring to is the inevitable gappy pre-Eschaton annihilation just discussed.

Returning to discussion of Matthew 25:41, this verse requires more analysis, in the broader context of Matthew 25. Consider the broader context of the verse:

> 40 And the King shall answer and say unto them, Verily I say unto you, Inasmuch as ye have done it unto one of the least of these my brethren, ye have done it unto me. 41 Then shall he say also unto them on the left hand, Depart from me, ye cursed, into everlasting fire, prepared for the devil and his angels: 42 for I was an hungred, and ye gave me no meat: I was thirsty, and ye gave me no drink: 43 I was a stranger, and ye took me not in: naked, and ye clothed me not: sick, and in prison, and ye visited me not. 44 Then shall they also answer him, saying, Lord, when saw we thee an hungred, or athirst, or a stranger, or naked, or sick, or in prison, and did not minister unto thee? 45 Then shall he answer them, saying, Verily I say unto you, Inasmuch as ye did it not to one of the least of these, ye did it not to me. 46 And these shall go away into everlasting punishment: but the righteous into life eternal. (Matt 25:40–46)

In verse 41, Jesus refers to the "everlasting fire," which is the Lake of Fire, since the fire of hell would not exist past the Eschaton ("heavens and earth pass away"), past the end of all things (1 Pet 4:7), and therefore hell is finite in duration, unlike the *Everlasting* Fire. There is only one unending Fire referred to in Scripture, which is GOD, who is revealed with Fire at the Eschaton. Then immediately Jesus traces back (verses 42–45) to pre-Eschaton times to discuss the lack of good works (faithful works). And then in verse 46 it is claimed that those of unfaithful works go into "everlasting punishment." There is no timeframe given for when this "everlasting punishment" is, but the "and" at the start of verse 46 ("And these shall go away into everlasting punishment . . .") tells us that verse 46 is a continuation of thought from verse 45, and therefore about the pre-Eschaton reality discussed in verses 42–45. For that reason, verse 46 is about pre-Eschaton "everlasting punishment," in the underworld reality, and the gap in the existence of the self. So, the "everlasting fire" of verse 41 is *not* identical to the "everlasting punishment" of verse 46. The everlastingness of annihilation punishment will be discussed in a chapter below, which will reveal why it

The Inevitable Gap of Annihilation Self-Nonexistence

is called "everlasting" and/or "eternal," when it is nevertheless reversed (the everlastingness and/or eternality are *interrupted*, by GOD) at the Eschaton.

9

Lazarus and the Beggar (Luke 16)

As for the Story of Lazarus and the Beggar in Luke 16:19–31, this is definitely the most widely mentioned passage I hear about when people tell me there is scriptural support for the popular and traditional view of hell. I contend that it is self-evident that the Story of Lazarus and the Beggar is a parable, for reasons explained in this chapter. But first, here is the passage:

> 19 There was a certain rich man, which was clothed in purple and fine linen, and fared sumptuously every day: 20 and there was a certain beggar named Lazarus, which was laid at his gate, full of sores, 21 and desiring to be fed with the crumbs which fell from the rich man's table: moreover the dogs came and licked his sores. 22 And it came to pass, that the beggar died, and was carried by the angels into Abraham's bosom: the rich man also died, and was buried; 23 and in hell he lift up his eyes, being in torments, and seeth Abraham afar off, and Lazarus in his bosom. 24 And he cried and said, Father Abraham, have mercy on me, and send Lazarus, that he may dip the tip of his finger in water, and cool my tongue; for I am tormented in this flame. 25 But Abraham said, Son, remember that thou in thy lifetime receivedst thy good things, and likewise Lazarus evil things: but now he is comforted, and thou art tormented. 26 And beside all this, between us and you there is a great gulf fixed: so that they which would pass from hence to you cannot; neither can they pass to us, that would come from thence. 27 Then he said, I pray thee therefore, father, that thou wouldest send him to my father's house: 28 for I have five brethren; that he may testify unto them, lest they also come into this place of torment. 29 Abraham saith unto him, They have Moses and the prophets; let them hear them. 30 And he said, Nay, father

Lazarus and the Beggar (Luke 16)

Abraham: but if one went unto them from the dead, they will repent. 31 And he said unto him, If they hear not Moses and the prophets, neither will they be persuaded, though one rose from the dead. (Luke 16:19–31)

The Story of Lazarus and the Beggar is in Luke, which is glutted with parables, and the Story of Lazarus and the beggar is located right in a long string of parables involving rich men and involving money and wealth (the Parables of Hidden Treasure, the Pearl, the Unforgiving Servant, Lost Coin, Prodigal Son, Unjust Steward, Master and Servant, to name some of them). The Story of Lazarus and the Beggar is the only story in the Bible that could be claimed to appear anything roughly like the popular view of hell (and it is not a perfect match). Therefore, the parable seems to be intended to be like the other parables in Luke, it was never meant to be taken as a story that actually happened, and therefore not to be taken as a description of the popular view of hell. From what I can tell, parables are of two types. Firstly, those that are to be taken as representations of fact, that stay close to the known physics and metaphysics of reality, meant to rather precisely describe actual reality. On an evangelical and literalist reading of Scripture, the Parable of the Tares would be a good example of this first type, and such parables are often taken not truly to be parables, but as accounts of reality, of things that *have* happened or *will* happen. But other parables, of the second sort, are less bound to remaining in line with our ideas of what reality is like. This second type may use alternative ideas of physics, for example—alternative to what is ordinarily believed reality and its laws or forces of nature are like (for example, the Parable of the Shrewd Manager, Luke 16:1–13). Apparently, the Parable of Lazarus and the Beggar is of the second type. The first sort are those that could be real, could be about real events, things that happened. The second group is not; they are more like stories of fantasy, things that are not meant to be taken as real, or that would or could happen. Rather, they are imaginary worlds, portrayed to show some specific theological points.

Furthermore, if the Parable of Lazarus and the Beggar were the first sort of parable involving more literal accounts of the physics and metaphysics of actual reality, and a situation that could have or did happen, then multiple contradictions would emerge between the Parable of Lazarus and the Beggar, on the one hand, and the rest of Scripture, on the other. For example, Scripture elsewhere indicates that in the afterlife we will not remember former things: "For, behold, I create new heavens and a new earth:

Hyper-Calvinist Universal Salvation

and the former shall not be remembered, nor come into mind" (Isa 65:17). This verse would be contradicted with the Story of Lazarus and the Beggar, if it were not a parable, and a parable of the second sort, since while in hell Lazarus appears to be fully cogent and conscious, for a long span of time, remembering former things: recalling elements from his life in the world.

It would appear that a second contradiction is found with how Lazarus is neither annihilated or asleep, which would contradict the plentiful amount of passages about the pre-Eschaton annihilation discussed above. Lazarus does not appear to be in a state of soul loss and self-nonexistence (soul dormancy). So, taking the Story of Lazarus and the Beggar as a parable of the second sort, for multiple reasons just listed, seems to be our only option.

Hyper-Calvinist universal salvation, described in biblical eschatology and soteriology, dissolves multiple paradoxes and absurdities that are falsely believed to exist in Scripture, such as how an all-loving GOD supposedly creates creatures (people) only to prevent them (Mark 4:12) from turning to the LORD (Luke 8:10; Isa 6:9–10), in order to torture them endlessly and in unfathomable horror, stemming from the corruption in their hearts *that they were created with* (1 Cor 15:42), outside of their control. I believe it is safe to say that the popular view of hell involves that contradiction, but Hyper-Calvinist universal salvation involves a thorough resolution to the situation. Other than the contradiction of the popular view of hell, there are other supposed paradoxes from incorrect popular, contemporary views, that would appear to be solved by the hyper-literalist scriptural theology of Hyper-Calvinist universal salvation (some of which are discussed in later chapters).

The limited atonement paradox may be an example. Scripture tells us in some verses that all are saved, and in other verses that not all are saved. This involves a scriptural contradiction if the two groups exist always at the same time. But Hyper-Calvinist universal salvation relies on Scripture to show that there is a two-step salvation process, where first the chosen are saved before the Eschaton (limited atonement), and then the unchosen are saved at the Eschaton (universal salvation). The condemned live before the Eschaton, but then things change at the Eschaton, where a reality of universal salvation commences. No contradiction.

This is the only passage in the Bible which mentions a fire torment in the underworld. But from what has been found about the parable in this chapter, this is the sort of parable that does not represent the physics and

Lazarus and the Beggar (Luke 16)

metaphysics of reality, and is instead meant to be taken as portraying a reality that is specifically not real. For this reason, we should expect the actual reality to be other than elements of the Parable of Lazarus and the Beggar, such as Hades being fiery, or that there is a fiery underworld of conscious torture. These should be anticipated as being about an imaginary world of fantasy.

10

Scriptural Support for Hyper-Calvinist Universal Salvation, Part 2

ACCORDING TO THE EVANGELICAL systematic theology of Hyper-Calvinist universal salvation, the Creator GOD created, in some initial way, all humans before the world was created (Eph 1:4), where he *specifically* created them *corrupted*.[1] And then he completes the activity of making them noncorrupted at the end of the world (1 Cor 15:42, 52)—and he does this by immersing them in his Consuming Fire (1 Cor 3:15; Mark 9:49; Heb 12:29), his Lake of Fire, which is the Eschaton. Scripture states that only *some*[2] humans are chosen and saved *before* the end of the world (the Eschaton), but GOD will save all remaining humans, that is, all unchosen

---

1. This is the topic of a chapter late in this book, but as an aside, I want to comment on the significance of this point now—that humans were created as *corrupted*. This is the only way anything can be created by a monotheistic Creator, if that Creator is the unblemished greatest conceivable being. Logically speaking, there can only be *one* such uncorrupted entity that can exist, which would be GOD only, and that being so, then if GOD creates anything *distinct* from himself, then it is corrupt, since he is the only uncorrupt. So, there is a mystery of how a corrupted thing can ultimately originate from an uncorrupt entity. This would be an argument for *creatio ex nihilo*: any corrupted created entity cannot come from the being or nature of the one uncorrupted Being. This is a *logical* principle, contained in the message of 1 Cor 15:42, and it explains why reality is how it is: a damaged (corrupted) reality that needs to be saved by its Creator, by becoming one with its Creator. I previously discussed this in Grupp, "Why God Did Not Choose All Souls," 17, and this would be the long-sought solution to the problem of evil, and the problem of pain (discussed in a chapter below). In a universe created by one GOD who is the one noncorrupt, anything created by GOD would be corrupted and need to unite with GOD, the one uncorrupted, in order to exist uncorrupted.

2. See Grupp, "Why God Did Not Choose All Souls," 116 (note 5).

Scriptural Support for Hyper-Calvinist Universal Salvation, Part 2

and condemned humans, *at the Eschaton*, by immersing them in the Lake of Fire, in his own Being, during the Fire Eschaton. So, reality contains a two-step salvation process:

1. Before the Eschaton, the few (Matt 22:14) elect, the chosen, are saved (pre-Eschaton), undergoing some sort of initial salvation, where they cannot see GOD as we will see him at the Eschaton (see 1 John 3:2; Rev 1:7), but in this pre-Eschaton salvation, the salvific *can* see GOD, experience him, *directly*, but in varying levels of imperfect comprehension—that is, as if seeing him through glass in a mysterious way, or perhaps in darkness (1 Cor 13:12).

2. At the Eschaton, the remainder of humans, the non-elect, are burned by GOD's Fire, in order to be saved (at the Eschaton) (1 Cor 3:15).

Only the non-elect will be hurt during this transformation at the Eschaton (see Rev 2:11[3]).

More verses and passages will be presented to support the thesis of Hyper-Calvinist universal salvation. Here are a few more:

> For God hath concluded them all in unbelief, that he might have mercy upon *all*. (Rom 11:32)

> That was the true Light, which *lighteth every man* that cometh into the world. (John 1:9)

> And *every creature which is in heaven, and on the earth, and under the earth*, and such as are in the sea, and all that are in them, heard I saying, Blessing, and honour, and glory, and power, be unto him that sitteth upon the throne, and unto the Lamb for ever and ever.[4] (Rev 5:13)

---

3. I interpret the second death (the death of death) to be coinciding in time, in the Lake of Fire, with the baptism of fire of the Eschaton. And I interpret the first death to be a t an earlier time, as becoming a being of fallenness with sin diseasing the human being at the fall of creation in the garden of Eden. The baptism of fire as being the Lake of Fire, the Consuming Fire, will be discussed and scripturally verified in a chapter below.

4. The verses surrounding this one make it appear that this verse is about a pre-Eschaton time, but also a time when the Eschaton is very near, and to such a degree that it is in some way commencing, during the time of the seven seals. So, the Eschaton is here, even though we cannot yet see its full final form. But nevertheless, this includes *every creature, even those under the earth* (John 5:28), which would include those coming *out of* their self-nonexistence. This would appear to indicate that the universalism is becoming actualized—at least in more-and-more widespread ways—slightly *before* the Eschaton. That is likely happening in the world today. We know that both (1) every creature is

Hyper-Calvinist Universal Salvation

The law and the prophets were until John: since that time the kingdom of God is preached, and *every* man presseth into it. (Luke 16:16)

Another parable spake he unto them; The kingdom of heaven is like unto leaven, which a woman took, and hid in three measures of meal, till *the whole* was leavened. (Matt 13:33)

For the bread of God is he which cometh down from heaven, and *giveth life unto the world*. (John 6:33)

O praise the Lord, *all* ye nations: praise him, *all* ye people. (Ps 117:1)

10 And, Thou, Lord, in the beginning hast laid the foundation of the earth; and the heavens are the works of thine hands: 11 they shall perish; but thou remainest; and they all shall wax old as doth a garment; 12 and as a vesture shalt thou fold them up, and they shall be changed: but thou art the same, and thy years shall not fail. (Heb 1:10-12)

A passage of Scripture that breaks down Hyper-Calvinist universal salvation is the Parable of the Tares in Matthew 13. In a chapter above, I discussed how some parables of Scripture appear to be about real events, whereas others are specifically not intended to represent anything in any reality. The Tares is of the first type. In the parable, it can be seen that there are two groups, the chosen and the unchosen, where the unchosen are

---

looking forward, into the Eschaton, and therein praising GOD (Rom 8:21-23), and (2), the Eschaton is reaching into the past to begin implanting its effects into all creatures, which means that this is happening now, as if the fire of the LORD is here now, burning us, or preparing us for burning (see 1 Thess 2:19 KJV wording only, and Luke 12:49; this multivariate topic is discussed elsewhere in this book, as it shows up multiple places in Scripture). This concept would lead to interesting conclusions, such as, to give an example, a person who is a committed and genuine atheist, today, will nevertheless, at some level into their soul, feel GOD, and perhaps have some moments of GOD speaking to them, and him giving them revelation. I know this happened to me in my twenties, when I was still a very fervent atheist, perhaps in my most convicted time as an atheist. Years after becoming a Christian, I remembered one notable case of these experiences, which happened one day as I was driving down the road in Albuquerque, New Mexico, where I lived when I was a student at the University of New Mexico in my twenties. This experience roughly blended in with the rest of my daily thought stream, but involved a consciousness that definitely stuck out as different, far more vivid, and the "thoughts" felt more like an encounter, or an invasion (takeover) in my mind during this time. But I believe I did not acknowledge the experiences for what they were, and I even wanted to deny them, since I was an atheist.

Scriptural Support for Hyper-Calvinist Universal Salvation, Part 2

blocked from believing (verses 10–15; we also see this blocking in Mark 4:12), indicating Hyper-Calvinism, even though they apparently otherwise could have or would have believed. And specifically at the very end (the Eschaton), the unchosen are burned, but there is no mention that the burned continue burning past this ending (beyond the Eschaton Lake of Fire event). *Instead*, with the way the passage flows, it is immediately *after* this burning, at the end, that the "righteous shine forth as the sun," a passage where Scripture indicates what humans will be when they are their true selves (when we are looking at GOD's face in the afterlife; see 1 John 3:2), since we will be like suns, spheres of blinding light, just like GOD, who is also a sun, a sphere of blinding light:

> For the LORD God is a sun and shield: the LORD will give grace and glory: no good thing will he withhold from them that walk uprightly. (Ps 84:11; also see Matt 17:2; Isa 9:2; and Mal 4:2)

At the very end of the Parable of the Tares, the Eschaton Fire is *directly adjacent to* and preceding the shining as the sun—as if one follows directly from the other in the sequence of events. Also consider this passage, about the sheep of the first resurrection:

> 2 And many of them that sleep in the dust of the earth shall awake, some to everlasting life, and some to shame and everlasting contempt.[5] 3 And they that be wise shall shine as the brightness of the firmament; and they that turn many to righteousness as the stars for ever and ever. (Dan 12:2–3)

According to the worldwide pop theology (the free will theology), the goats will be put in hell (in accord to the fallacious popular view of hell), and I believe it is the following verse, from the book of Revelation, about the second death (which does not mention *hell*) that is used to generate that false idea:

> But the fearful, and unbelieving, and the abominable, and murderers, and whoremongers, and sorcerers, and idolaters, and all liars, shall have their part in the lake which burneth with fire and brimstone: which is the second death. (Rev 21:8)

I will deal with this passage in fine detail in a chapter below, but to give a hint of what we will discover regarding this verse, it does not mention hell and is not about hell (it is about the Lake of Fire, which is YHWH/Θεός), and this "second death" is not a death of people, since the chapter

---

5. This concept of "everlasting contempt" is dealt with in detail in a chapter below.

before (Rev 20:14–15) refers to death dying (death ends, which I will call "the death of death" in a chapter below) in the second death, and it does not mention people dying, so therefore, if death is destroyed in the second death, then the people in the second death cannot also be destroyed, since there will be no death there to destroy them. Instead, the second death is about the Baptism of Fire:

> Who shall change our vile body, that it may be fashioned like unto his glorious body, according to the working whereby he is able even to subdue *all things* unto himself. (Phil 3:21; also see Eccl 12:7; 1 Cor 5:5; Rom 14:8; Gal 2:20; John 11:25)

There cannot be annihilation and/or torture in hell if God reconciles (Acts 3:21; Col 1:20–21) and subdues all things to himself. This is why Revelation 21:8 does not mention people dying, but rather it only mentions that the second death happens, which we were already very clearly informed is the death of death (20:14), not the death of people. An entire chapter below is dedicated to this specific topic.

Back to the Parable of the Tares: if the reader did not have an assumption that the fire was the popular view of hell (rather than being the Lake of Fire/GOD), the Parable of the Tares could be seen for what it is: a representation of the Eschaton Fire (Lake of Fire), a transition from Eschaton Fire directly to afterlife in GOD's light. A *never-ending* torment, such as seen with the popular view of hell, is not mentioned, and therefore is, strictly speaking, not involved with those who are tares (the unchosen) in this parable. There is no mention of fire destroying them, or any tortuous hell-like activity; only that they were in fire, and then they were in the new reality of the afterlife. And juxtapose this passage with Luke 20:37–38: "the dead are raised . . . for he is not a God of the dead, but of the living: for all live unto him," which is a passage specifically about the Eschaton, where some or all of the universally saved will even be "equal to angels" (Luke 20:36). "The dead," which at the very least would include all the unsaved, are raised, and therefore only can be alive ("for he is not a God of the dead, but of the living: for *all* live unto him"; Luke 20:38). This is blatantly proclaiming universal salvation, and universal salvation at the Eschaton Fire—the Eschaton Light (also see Rev 22:5) referred to at the end of the Parable of the Tares. The chosen and unchosen, altogether, comprise all human beings of earth that were ever created—no human being of earth would fall outside that logical dichotomy—and for that reason, we know from verse 30 of the Parable of the Tares that all people, all the chosen and unchosen, *before the Eschaton,*

Scriptural Support for Hyper-Calvinist Universal Salvation, Part 2

comprise one cooperative, one system ("both grow together"), almost as if we should expect the two groups to comingle in some sort of deep way, and to mix their *roots*, together all moving through time, while in their corrupted state, toward and into the afterlife of the Eschaton (1 Cor 15:42). After discussion of the Parable of the Tares, we will discuss John 10, and where John 10:16 explicitly refers to the oneness of humanity, as one group, one fold, where those who are not part of the herd are brought into the one flock, but where this happens seemingly at a final time, and therefore *at the Eschaton*. So, in the Parable of the Tares, at the end, where humanity is directly with GOD, that can only mean all of humanity, the living and the dead, who will be *all* drawn into GOD (John 12:32) for the afterlife forever. And right after Jesus' discussion of the Parable of the Tares, we find in Matthew 13:33 the claim that the kingdom of heaven is worked through "the whole," in the next parable listed in Scripture, in a verse immediately adjacent to the end of the Parable of the Tares, putting the Parable of the Tares right in the context of discussion of parables where the kingdom of heaven reaches into *all* of humanity (universal salvation). Here is the full passage, including verse 13:33:

> 10 And the disciples came, and said unto him, Why speakest thou unto them in parables? 11 He answered and said unto them, Because it is given unto you to know the mysteries of the kingdom of heaven, but to them it is not given. 12 For whosoever hath, to him shall be given, and he shall have more abundance: but whosoever hath not, from him shall be taken away even that he hath. 13 Therefore speak I to them in parables: because they seeing see not; and hearing they hear not, neither do they understand. 14 And in them is fulfilled the prophecy of Esaias, which saith, By hearing ye shall hear, and shall not understand; and seeing ye shall see, and shall not perceive: 15 for this people's heart is waxed gross, and their ears are dull of hearing, and their eyes they have closed; lest at any time they should see with their eyes, and hear with their ears, and should understand with their heart, and should be converted, and I should heal them... 24 Another parable put he forth unto them, saying, The kingdom of heaven is likened unto a man which sowed good seed in his field: 25 but while men slept, his enemy came and sowed tares among the wheat, and went his way. 26 But when the blade was sprung up, and brought forth fruit, then appeared the tares also. 27 So the servants of the householder came and said unto him, Sir, didst not thou sow good seed in thy field? from whence then hath it tares? 28 He said unto them, An

enemy hath done this. The servants said unto him, Wilt thou then that we go and gather them up? 29 But he said, Nay; lest while ye gather up the tares, ye root up also the wheat with them. 30 Let both grow together until the harvest: and in the time of harvest I will say to the reapers, Gather ye together first the tares, and bind them in bundles to burn them: but gather the wheat into my barn. 31 Another parable put he forth unto them, saying, The kingdom of heaven is like to a grain of mustard seed, which a man took, and sowed in his field: 32 which indeed is the least of all seeds: but when it is grown, it is the greatest among herbs, and becometh a tree, so that the birds of the air come and lodge in the branches thereof. 33 Another parable spake he unto them; The kingdom of heaven is like unto leaven, which a woman took, and hid in three measures of meal, till *the whole* was leavened. 34 All these things spake Jesus unto the multitude in parables; and without a parable spake he not unto them: 35 that it might be fulfilled which was spoken by the prophet, saying, I will open my mouth in parables; I will utter things which have been kept secret from the foundation of the world. 36 Then Jesus sent the multitude away, and went into the house: and his disciples came unto him, saying, Declare unto us the parable of the tares of the field. 37 He answered and said unto them, He that soweth the good seed is the Son of man; 38 the field is the world; the good seed are the children of the kingdom; but the tares are the children of the wicked one; 39 the enemy that sowed them is the devil; the harvest is the end of the world; and the reapers are the angels. 40 As therefore the tares are gathered and burned in the fire; so shall it be in the end of this world. 41 The Son of man shall send forth his angels, and they shall gather out of his kingdom all things that offend, and them which do iniquity; 42 and shall cast them into a furnace of fire: there shall be wailing and gnashing of teeth. 43 Then shall the righteous shine forth as the sun in the kingdom of their Father. Who hath ears to hear, let him hear. (Matt 13:10–15, 24–43)

This phenomenon, where the furnace is *directly* adjacent to, and *directly* followed by, the kingdom of the sun, without any mention of the condemned dying or being destroyed or tortured, is a pattern that repeats in Scripture, as will be pointed out in other chapters. The gnashing of teeth referred to at the end, I have often been told, is a reference to the popular view of hell, and therefore people being thrown into hell—but that cannot be correct, as this is about the very end of the world, the end of all things (note that a few lines up it says, "so shall it be at the end of this world. The

Scriptural Support for Hyper-Calvinist Universal Salvation, Part 2

Son of man shall send forth his angels . . . ," which is referring to Eschaton events). So, this burning is a reference to the Lake of Fire, which below we will find is GOD and his Eschaton Fire, and that is why this gnashing of teeth verse is directly followed by this: "Then shall the righteous shine forth as the sun in the kingdom of their Father."

Another passage that communicates Hyper-Calvinist universalist salvation is in John 10. In this well-known passage,[6] we again see a demarcation between the chosen and unchosen, the saved and the condemned (where the chosen and unchosen comprise all human beings), where no human beings fall outside of this group. But then at a later time, *after* this demarcation was set, GOD saves all the rest of the sheep, so there is only one Shepherd and one fold. In other words, currently there are the chosen and the unchosen, but in the future *all* will be brought into GOD's *one flock* (that is, the unchosen will be saved). This is the thesis of Hyper-Calvinist universal salvation. Here is the passage:

> 1 Verily, verily, I say unto you, He that entereth not by the door into the sheepfold, but climbeth up some other way, the same is a thief and a robber. 2 But he that entereth in by the door is the shepherd of the sheep. 3 To him the porter openeth; and the sheep hear his voice: and he calleth his own sheep by name, and leadeth them out. 4 And when he putteth forth his own sheep, he goeth before them, and the sheep follow him: for they know his voice... 6 This parable spake Jesus unto them: but they understood not what things they were which he spake unto them. 7 Then said Jesus unto them again, Verily, verily, I say unto you, I am the door of the sheep. 8 All that ever came before me are thieves and robbers: but the sheep did not hear them. 9 I am the door: by me if any man enter in, he shall be saved, and shall go in and out, and find pasture... 11 I am the good shepherd: the good shepherd giveth his life for the sheep. 12 But he that is an hireling, and not the shepherd, whose own the sheep are not, seeth the wolf coming, and leaveth the sheep, and fleeth: and the wolf catcheth them, and scattereth the sheep. 13 The hireling fleeth, because he is an hireling, and careth not for the sheep. 14 I am the good shepherd, and know my sheep, and am known of mine. 15 As the Father knoweth me, even so know I the Father: and I lay down my life for the sheep. 16 And other sheep I have, which are not of this fold: them also I must

---

6. Actually, it probably best to say that it is well known only up to verse 15. Verse 16 and to the end I find not widely discussed (from what I can tell), and the blatantly universalist aspects of the passage that start in verse 16.

Hyper-Calvinist Universal Salvation

> bring, and they shall hear my voice; *and there shall be one fold*, and one shepherd. 17 Therefore doth my Father love me, because I lay down my life, that I might take it again. (John 10:1–4, 6–9, 11–17)

Note again how the italicized phrase from John 10:16 involves the universal saving as being future. The Parable of the Tares is also future-pointing, a very consistent theme of the omnisalvation of humanity that will occur at the Eschaton.

Discovering Hyper-Calvinist universal salvation permeating Scripture should not be surprising, since Scripture plainly tells us that the underworld realm of the dead (Hades, hell) *will not last forever* (Mark 13:31; Rev 20:14; more Scripture cited below), and also that all things *will be* (in the future) restored (Acts 3:21; Col 1:20; 2 Cor 5:19). I find it hard to avoid directly concluding that a passage like John 10 points to Hyper-Calvinist universal salvation theology as being the theology that is scriptural.

Above we saw how some widely discussed verses (such as "every knee shall bow") in fact contain Hyper-Calvinist universal salvation, or even the two stages of salvation in Hyper-Calvinist universal salvation, but where that has not been recognized. Below are samples of more verses and passages that are widely discussed, and which involve Hyper-Calvinist universal salvation. And notice, again, in these widely discussed passages, the *future*-pointing nature of some of these examples, where all are *not* saved *now* (there are condemned *and* unsaved presently), but where universal salvation is future, not present, at the future Eschaton Fire.

> 8 And there were in the same country shepherds abiding in the field, keeping watch over their flock by night. 9 And, lo, the angel of the Lord came upon them, and the glory of the Lord shone round about them: and they were sore afraid. 10 And the angel said unto them, Fear not: for, behold, I bring you good tidings of great joy, which *shall be to all people*. 11 For unto you is born this day in the city of David a Saviour, which is Christ the Lord. 12 And this *shall be* a sign unto you; Ye shall find the babe wrapped in swaddling clothes, lying in a manger. (Luke 2:8–12)
>
> 25 Verily, verily, I say unto you, The hour is coming, and now is,[7] when *the dead shall hear* the voice of the Son of God: and *they that*

---

[7]. In a footnote above, I discussed how some passages cited in this book seem to indicate that the universal salvation of the end (future) is, somehow, *also* reaching back, for lack of better words, into the present (pre-Eschaton), as this passages also indicates, where the Eschaton "is coming," but also "now is." This represents an alternative philosophy of time, and a chapter below is dedicated to this topic. This passage indicates that not

hear shall live. 26 For as the Father hath life in himself; so hath he given to the Son to have life in himself; 27 and hath given him authority to execute judgment also, because he is the Son of man. 28 Marvel not at this: for the hour is coming, in the which all that are in the graves shall hear his voice. (John 5:25–28)

The next day John seeth Jesus coming unto him, and saith, Behold the Lamb of God, which taketh away the sin of the world. (John 1:29)

22 For we know that *the whole creation* groaneth and travaileth in pain together until now. 23 And not only *they*, but ourselves also, which have the firstfruits of the Spirit, even we ourselves groan within ourselves, *waiting for* the adoption, *to wit*, the redemption of our body. (Rom 8:22–23)

Consider the following additional, lesser-discussed verses, which point to Hyper-Calvinist universal salvation, and where again some also reveal the two-step salvation dynamic: first there is pre-Eschaton Hyper-Calvinist double predestination (up to the Eschaton), and secondly, at a later point, in the future, there is total and maximal universalism (omnisalvation of both chosen and unchosen), which happens via the Eschaton Fire. I have again italicized the future-pointing aspects of these Hyper-Calvinist universal salvation passages below:

Whom the heaven must receive *until the times* of restitution *of all things*, which God hath spoken by the mouth of all his holy prophets since the world began. (Acts 3:21)

And he is the propitiation for our sins: and not for ours only, but also for the sins of the whole world. (1 John 2:2)

Therefore as by the offence of one judgment came upon all men to condemnation; even so by the righteousness of one the free gift came upon all men unto justification of life. (Rom 5:18)

13 every man's work *shall be made* manifest: for the day *shall declare* it, because it *shall be revealed by fire*; and the fire *shall try* every man's work of what sort it is. 14 If any man's work abide which he hath built thereupon, he *shall receive* a reward. 15 If any man's work *shall be burned*, he shall suffer loss: but he himself *shall be saved*; yet so as by fire. (1 Cor 3:13–15)

---

only will the dead hear GOD's voice at the Eschaton, but furthermore, the dead are *now*, presently, in some way, hearing his voice, as well. A chapter is devoted to this topic below.

Hyper-Calvinist Universal Salvation

For the bread of God is he which cometh down from heaven, and giveth life unto the world. (John 6:33)

And it shall come to pass, that from one new moon to another, and from one sabbath to another, *shall all flesh* come to worship before me, saith the Lord. (Isa 66:23)

For as in Adam all die, even so in Christ *shall all[8] be made alive.* (1 Cor 15:22)

For *in that day* every man *shall* cast away his idols of silver, and his idols of gold, which your own hands have made unto you for a sin. (Isa 31:7)

The glory of the LORD *shall be* revealed, and all flesh *shall see it* together: for the mouth of the LORD hath spoken it. (Isa 40:5)

For the Lord *will not cast off for ever.* (Lam 3:31)

Who *will have*[9] all men to be saved, and to come unto the knowledge of the truth. (1 Tim 2:4)

---

8. I have heard Chris Date, a present-day proponent of traditional annihilation (unending/permanent annihilation post-Eschaton, rather than the temporary annihilation pre-Eschaton discussed above; Date's view basically replaces the popular view of hell with annihilation), discuss how the "all" here, he claims, does not mean all people, but rather, all *types* of people. Date claims that virtually every universalist passage in the Bible that seems to refer to all people, such as Romans 5:18, actually does not refer to all people, and instead refers to all *types* of people. But I claim this is false, since there is no mention of *types, kinds, subgroups,* and so forth, in passages like this, and thus they can only mean *totality,* no exceptions, since that is the definition of the word "all." Date is trying to say that all ≠ all in order to argue for traditional post-Eschaton annihilation theology. If GOD meant "all types," then why wouldn't he have just written that, instead of being tricky, and writing *all*, when all did not really mean *all*. In order for Date's claim to be upheld, there would have to be Scripture that claimed that all the universalist passages that use "every" (1 Cor 4:5), "all," and so forth, are miswritten and actually mean every type, or all types. I maintain there is none, and thus the passages only can mean what they plainly say, they are referring to the totality.

9. I have been told that "will have" should be translated with the very different phrase "wants to." I have not seen the argument for why that is the case. I find it interesting that translating "will have," rather than "wants to," occurs only in the Textus-based Bibles and the pre-Textus Bibles in English: WYC, YTL, KJV, GNV, Tyndale Bible (Coverdale Bible, Matthew's Bible), The Great Bible 1539, Bishop's Bible 1568, Noah Webster 1833, Julia E. Smith 1876, with the exception of Green's Literal Translation (which is arguably not properly classified as an ancient translation). All of these use the same concept: that GOD *will save all* (a future universalist event). And on the other hand, all post-Textus translations, to my knowledge, do not use "will have," and instead use "wants all." But for all of the translations, the most ancient to most modern Bibles, all are translated from identical

Scriptural Support for Hyper-Calvinist Universal Salvation, Part 2

For therefore we both labour and suffer reproach, because we trust in the living God, who is the Saviour of all men, specially of those that believe.[10] (1 Tim 4:10)

Greek for 1 Tim 2:4, since there are no discrepancies regardless of which manuscript they were translated from—whether the 1550 Textus Receptus, the Byzantine Majority, the Alexandrian, the Hort and Westcott, and so on: all are identical. So, all Textus and pre-Textus translations agree with each other, translating 1 Tim 2:4 as GOD saving all in the future, and the post-Textus translations agree with each other, in translating 1 Tim 2:4 as GOD merely *wanting to* save all—but these two groups (Textus/pre-Textus versus post-Textus) disagree, which is quite interesting. How this change happened in translating 1 Tim 2:4 from the way the ancient group did, to the way the modern group has, is not explored in this book outside of this footnote, where I will consider the Textus and pre-Textus translations to be doctrinally sound, and the pre-Textus "wants to" to be doctrinally problematical, to the point of leading to a contradiction in the post-Textus translations that does not exist in the Textus and pre-Textus translations. The Textus and pre-Textus "will have" fits far better into the overall plan of Scripture (which is Hyper-Calvinist universal salvation), and it avoids the unsettling paradox that the omnipotent Creator-GOD *cannot* save all people—he only wants to, but won't, or can't, do what he wants, and he can't have what he wants.

But there is a much larger point to explore surrounding this matter. To get to the point, consider Ps 115:3: "But our God is in the heavens: he hath done whatsoever he hath pleased" (AKJV), "God . . . does whatever pleases him" (NIV), "God . . . does all that he pleases" (ESV). So, if one claims that GOD *wants to* save all people, *but does not*, a contradiction emerges in Scripture: GOD does what he wants *and* does not do what he wants. This contradiction is avoided by interpreting "wants to" in the modern Bibles in a way where GOD *did*, in fact, do what he wants according to 1 Tim 2:4. But this would mean he *has saved all people*, since in the post-Textus Bibles, 1 Tim 2:4 reads that GOD wants to save all; so if he wanted to save all, then all can only be saved, due to Ps 115:3. And furthermore, this means that the "wants to" in the post-Textus translation merely reduces to the "will have" of the earlier/ancient translations, wherein the ancient translations are more accurate, since the post-Textus translations do not involve the more direct and revealing "will have. If this is not the case—that GOD has saved *all*—then a contradiction emerges in the doctrine of the newer (post-Textus) translations: GOD get anything he wants and does not get what he wants. Perhaps this is why the KJV involves the future-pointing, Eschaton-oriented, "will have," because Tyndale and his team were made aware of the issues just discussed. Some may assert that despite all of this, all still will *not* be saved, since humans may respond to GOD with free will and reject Him, choosing to not be saved. But this would be to deny Ps 115:3 as true, and to deny GOD's omnipotence in saving all people if he merely wants to (which the post-Textus translations say he does), and further, there are problems with believing that GOD's desire is not strong enough to overtake a human's supposed resistance. In general, if GOD is sovereign, such human response matters not.

10. This verse seems to imply there are two groups of saved people. In other words, all people are saved, but there are two subgroups that all people comprise. And the way the verse is written, it is as if one group is more blessed in salvation than the other. This would fit consistently with Heb 6:9, which indicates that some salvation is better than others.

Hyper-Calvinist Universal Salvation

49 For *every one shall be salted with fire*, and every sacrifice *shall be salted with salt.* 50 Salt *is* good: but if the salt have lost his saltness, wherewith will ye season it? Have salt in yourselves, and have peace one with another. (Mark 9:49–50)

These verses reveal the *two-step* salvific process of Hyper-Calvinist universal salvation, where before the Eschaton there are both the saved and condemned, and then at the Eschaton *all*[11] are burned by, or at least affected by, the Consuming Fire (see Mark 9:49) at the Eschaton, the Lake of Fire, wherein, secondly, all remaining unsaved are saved. The absolutely dominant never-get-out-of-hell view is plainly not found in Scripture.

---

11. Both Rev 2:11 and Rev 20:6 state that the uncondemned are not hurt in the Lake of Fire event at the end of all things.

11

Free Will and the Popular View of Hell

USUALLY WHEN PEOPLE TALK to me about universalism, they have very few concepts about it to work with, but one they seem to always have is that universalism means that there is no hell. I do not know how this view could fit into an evangelical systematic theology, since hell is denoted in Scripture many times, and therefore it exists (though not in accord with the traditional view of hell). One place that the popular view of hell and the scriptural account of hell differ is that in the scriptural account, no human being is ever burned in hell. The *popular* view of hell does not have commonalities with the scriptural accounts of the underworld regions—not only hell, but also Hades and Sheol, and Tartarus. That *popular* view of hell, which is seemingly endorsed worldwide, is tied to the non-scriptural concept of free will:

> The Popular View of Hell: Those who do not choose Jesus via their free will, while living in the physical domain, will be kept conscious to be tortured in the horrific burning of the fires of the hell underworld, forever, in a literal mathematical infinity of time, with no chance of escape or release out of hell torture ever offered: they will never leave, and will always remain in the maximally intense absolute state of torment at the height of total immolation, for a literal mathematical infinity of unending time—always and forever screaming in most horrific pain—where the all-loving Creator GOD caused and created this situation, and has turned his back on these condemned souls, separating himself from them.[1]

---

1. It is a contradiction to say that the most infinitely loving Creator GOD created this situation. For example, if a person commits the most heinous crime in this life, while in this physical world, and it causes unfathomable pain to multitudes of victims (Hitler

Hyper-Calvinist Universal Salvation

Before we analyze the popular view of hell further, let me say an initial point about free will, a concept (and I will argue a non-scriptural concept) that the popular view of hell depends on: since GOD does not do the sin, then humans must do it, in a mind event (free will event), not caused by GOD (in violation of the plethora of verses in Scripture that state GOD creates all). Hyper-Calvinist universal salvation does not require or involve human free will choice for salvation, and one cannot, for example, choose to stay condemned at the Eschaton. From Scripture, it appears that GOD will force all to be saved:

> And other sheep I have, which are not of this fold: them also I must bring, and they shall hear my voice; and there shall be one fold, and one shepherd. (John 10:16)

It seems that, with a verse like this, the concept of free will becomes superfluous; an abstraction at best, and a contradiction at worst.

As with John 10:16, there are widespread indications in Scripture of GOD overriding any choice a human has. For example, in Psalm 23:4, we see that GOD *makes* a person lie down ("He *maketh* me to lie down in green pastures . . ."). To give another example, Ezekiel 36:27: "And I will put my spirit within you, *and cause you* to walk in my statutes, and ye shall keep my judgments, and do them." Philosophers widely conclude that human free will is self-contradictory.[2] And it has been widely discussed how supposed free will decisions conflict with the sovereignty of GOD: if my life,

---

would be the classic example), this pain would only exist for a *finite amount of time*, and would indeed end, such as when a person arrived in the afterlife on the New Earth. But the person in hell, according to the popular view of hell just defined, would undergo at least equally painful torture (if not even more painful) for an infinite amount of time—so, the punishment would be infinitely long temporally, for causing pain that was only finitely long temporally. In simpler terms: the punishment is *infinitely greater* than the pain it caused. Perhaps if the punishment was in some *finite* way greater than the pain, it could be argued that was a logical scenario, but infinitely greater punishment seems to result in a contradiction: the maximally just GOD created a situation of maximal injustice. How can infinite injustice come from a Being who is infinitely just? If the pain caused by the terror is represented by one grain of sand, the punishment would be represented not just by an entire beach of sand, but by an infinity of beaches of sand. How can infinite wetness lead to infinite dryness, by analogy? How can a finite event be matched with an infinite one, like saying one ripe apple can have some sort of comparison to an infinity of infinities of mountains of fly-infested rotten apples? One apple is finite in time, but the infinities of piles are without end: mathematically everlasting. I find that "comparison" to lead to contradiction: finitude cannot produce infinitude.For example, see For example, seeFor example, see

2. Van Inwagen, "Powers of Rational Beings," 430–31.

Free Will and the Popular View of Hell

at this moment, is a product of all my decisions (free will decisions), and your life is for you, and every other person in the world for their life, then GOD seems a bit irrelevant, like a passive GOD that does not have much control. This starkly conflicts with Scripture, which states that GOD is the Creator of all things (Rev 4:11), which would then include any aspect of the inner mind, which GOD also would have to create, just as Scripture says he created our inner minds:

> 39 And the Lord said unto him, Now do ye Pharisees make clean the outside of the cup and the platter; but your inward part is full of ravening and wickedness. 40 Ye fools, did not he that made that which is without make that which is within also? (Luke 11:39–40)

Free will theology, from what I can tell, did not emerge with the life of Jesus, or from Scripture laying down any sort of human free will theology. Rather, it emerged in the second century, after Jesus, and not with the emergence of Scripture. Karamanolis writes:

> The notions of free will and divine providence are as central in the thought of early Christian philosophers as they are for their Hellenic contemporaries... By the time of Justin Martyr, Christians are already exhibiting a strong interest in the issue of free will and in the role of divine providence... If we look at Scripture, however, either the Old or the New Testament, we do not find a discussion of this kind... The Scriptures not only lack a relevant discussion but also lack the concepts and the terms that Christian philosophers employ when discussing the issue of free will, such as that something is up to us..., that we are masters of our choices ..., and that we have the power to choose freely.[3]

Free will can be identified as an early church philosophy, and not as a scriptural concept.

Karamanolis further discusses how there "are statements that bear on the issue of free will, such as that of Jesus, who wishes he could avoid suffering but follows his Father's willing..."[4] If this were correct, it must be noted that Karamanolis is discussing GOD (Jesus), not the rest of humanity, and therefore Karamanolis's comment does not help with understanding *ordinary human* free will choice. GOD (Jesus) *does* have free will, since, being GOD, he can do what he wants (Ps 115:3), and he can create things, and create them out of nothing, as a free will moment would seem to involve.

---

3. Karamanolis, *Philosophy of Early Christianity*, 144–45.
4. Karamanolis, *Philosophy of Early Christianity*, 144.

Hyper-Calvinist Universal Salvation

But that is different from an ordinary (non-GOD) creature, rather than Christ, who is the GOD-man.

Much Scripture may appear to be about human free will (for example, "seek the LORD with all your heart . . ."), but regardless of any such verse, Jesus says apart from him we can do nothing (John 15:5), where any work in us starts with GOD (Isa 26:12 KJV wording only; Phil 1:6), so it would appear any apparent free will act would in fact be GOD working in humans, and not a work starting from the human will. And lastly, I do not know of any Scripture, in any translation, ancient or modern, which discusses human free will at any length. If GOD is the Creator of all things (Rev 4:11), then I do not see how humans can create free will moments inside their consciousness. And the idea that humans can share in the free will of GOD seems difficult to argue when, as we just saw, all good works first originate from GOD (Phil 1:6), and not from humans.

As a brief aside, in the passage from Karamanolis above, he indicates that the quote from Jesus is about him wanting to avoid suffering, and essentially avoid the cross. This an apparently widespread position, involving the concept that Jesus wanted to avoid the cross. I believe this is an incorrect interpretation of these passages, since if Jesus wanted to avoid the cross, he would have gotten what he wanted (Ps 115:3), and if Jesus did not die on the cross, then no humans could have salvation (1 Cor 15:13–14). And it seems that the passages about passing the cup are about Jesus' body:

> And he went a little further, and fell on his face, and prayed, saying, O my Father, if it be possible, let this cup pass from me: nevertheless not as I will, but as thou wilt. (Matt 26:39)

If one looks carefully at this passage, it appears that it is about the activity, or the movement, of a cup (let this body pass from me), rather than the avoidance of suffering. This is quite significant, because the cup, or the vessel, a mold *formed* and shaped by GOD out of *unformed* clay by the riverbed (see Dan 2:43 KJV wording), in Scripture, represents the human person, the temple of GOD (many passages could be cited, such as Jer 18:4 and Rom 9:19–23, to name just two), a vessel which is in-filled with contents, by the omnicausal Creator GOD (see Luke 11:39–40, a passage which describes the body as the cup). Interpreting this passage in this way (rather than by the avoidance of suffering interpretation) is also in seeming accord with another verse that is often viewed as mysterious, but logical in this context, which is the following:

Free Will and the Popular View of Hell

> We are confident, I say, and willing rather to be absent from the body, and to be present with the Lord. (2 Cor 5:8)

Going back to discussion of hell, scripturally, hell is a rather multifaceted concept, but in the verses I cite below, hell is an *underworld*. Consider the following verses, which reveal the scriptural account of hell and/or Hades,[5] which has key distinctions from the popular view of hell, as well as distinctions from the Valley of Hinnon.

> And death and hell were cast into the lake of fire. This is the second death.[6] (Rev 20:14)

> For great is thy mercy toward me: and thou hast delivered my soul from the lowest hell.[7] (Ps 86:13)

> Because thou wilt not leave my soul in hell . . .[8] (Acts 2:27–29)

Launonen refers to the popular view as "the traditional view."[9] "Tertullian, Augustine, Aquinas, Luther, Calvin, and Wesley were all traditionalists, as were most of their contemporaries . . . Eternal conscious torment is also affirmed in the Athanasian Creed as well as many other confessions of various historical and contemporary churches."[10] I will not conjecture on how or why the popular view of hell and the underworld regions, being the inverse of *scriptural* account, came to be the dominant view, while the scriptural account is basically undiscussed.

---

5. These three verses are translated as Hades rather than hell in the newer translations. Hades is the land of the dead, which is underground.

6. This verse is not future-pointing, like other Scripture is, pointing to salvation being completed at the Eschaton in the future, and that is because it involves John's vision and revelation, in the book of Revelation, would have been experienced present tense, which is how John recorded it when the LORD had Him write it down when the book of Revelation was written.

7. More recent translations use "Sheol," or "depths of Sheol."

8. More recent translations use "Hades," as do some Textus-based Bibles, such as the Young Literal Translation.

9. Launonen, "Hell and the Cultural Evolution of Christianity," 194.

10. Launonen, "Hell and the Cultural Evolution of Christianity," 194.

12

GOD (YHWH, Θεός) = Lake of Fire, Part 2

IN THIS CHAPTER, I will show that, according to Scripture, the Lake of Fire *is identical to* GOD. And further, it can be shown that the Lake of Fire (GOD) is also the Eschaton Fire at the end of the physical world, at the end of all things (1 Pet 4:7). In other words, I will show that the Lake of Fire *is equal to* salvific Eschaton immolation in GOD (Christ), where the body is burned away, and spirit is saved unto salvation by Fire (1 Cor 3:12–15; 5:5). To my knowledge, these biblical points have been missed by theologians up to this point.

We know that GOD is equal to the Lake of Fire because Scripture is very specific on the qualities of each. Consider this deductive syllogism, which proves that GOD is identical to the Lake of Fire:

1. Only GOD can end death.
2. The Lake of Fire ends death.
3. Therefore GOD = the Lake of Fire.

According to *popular* theology (not the theology of this book), at the Eschaton resurrection there is then a *second* death, where people are judged, and those who did not use their free will during their life in the physical dimension to choose the real God are killed by that God in a *second* death, which is an eternal death of the self consisting of eternal conscious torture in fire (lake of fire, which is hell). That is the popular view, not the scriptural view. I do not know of any scripture that contains those elements of the popular theology, to thereby backup the popular theology with urgently needed scriptural support. And the scriptural view for what happens at the

GOD (YHWH, Θεός) = Lake of Fire, Part 2

Eschaton resurrection is *remarkably different* than this popular view, to the point that it becomes mysterious, in my opinion, that such differing views in the popular theology could have developed, and are now worldwide. It seems to me so mysterious that theologians have overlooked Hyper-Calvinist universal salvation theology for the past two millennia, given its obviousness in Scripture, that I feel I can only explain it by again resorting to how Scripture informs us that the minds of men are blinded from understanding the ways of GOD, which I have already discussed.

To come to the uncomplicated and elementary discovery that the Lake of Fire is identical to GOD, we will further compare Revelation 20:14 and Isaiah 25:8. If one looks at Revelation 20:14 for precisely what it is most plainly stating, it states that at the second death, which is the death at the Eschaton, it is at that point that *death itself*—and apparently *any and all death*—will be put into the Lake of Fire, and will perish: *the death of death*. We also find this in First Corinthians:

> 24 Then cometh the end, when he shall have delivered up the kingdom to God, even the Father; when he shall have put down all rule and all authority and power. 25 For he must reign, till he hath put all enemies under his feet. 26 *The last enemy that shall be destroyed is death.* (1 Cor 15:24–26)

This is a very important passage for Hyper-Calvinist universal salvation, since it tells us that at the end, death is destroyed. And, importantly, the verse right before Revelation 20:14 (Revelation 20:13: "death and hell delivered up the dead which were in them"), indicates that any people who were in hell are released from hell. Revelation 20:13 is the only verse in the KJV that says any people are in hell, and it does not say they are burning— instead, *it says they will be released from hell.*[1] The only verse in Scripture (KJV) to mention people in hell is a verse specifically about how any and all people that are in hell are to be *released* from hell! For these reasons just stated, that is how we know that what is precisely going on in Revelation 20:14 is that death *is being reversed*: a *death of death*. First, all the nonburning who are in hell are released from hell (v13), and then apparently

---

1. An argument could be made that Luke 10:15 is also a reference to people in hell (in the future) in the King James Bible, but in the original text in the Textus Receptus and the later-used documents (Hort and Westcott, Codex Vaticanus, etc.), it is Hades (ᾅδου), there is no mention of any burning of people in hell, and regardless, those of Capernaum will be released from hell at the Eschaton (Rev 20:13), right before death and hell are cast in the Lake of GOD-Fire.

Hyper-Calvinist Universal Salvation

shortly after this, hell is destroyed (v14); nobody will be in hell when it will be destroyed. This is not a death in hell, since hell has been destroyed, but this is the *death of death*, which is confirmed a few verses later in Revelation 21:4: "There shall be no more death."

Some claim that there "shall be no more death" *not* because death has been destroyed, and thus there cannot be any more death, but rather, because all the condemned have been subject to death already, and therefore there is not any more death. But there are multiple problems with that position. First, there are no verses that state anything like that in Scripture—that state that there is no more death because no condemned people are left to continue killing (annihilating or putting into eternal hell torture). Instead, we find Scripture about GOD *not* casting off his enemies:

> 29 He putteth his mouth in the dust; if so be there may be hope. 30 He giveth his cheek to him that smiteth him: he is filled full with reproach. 31 For the LORD will not cast off for ever: 32 but though he cause grief, yet will he have compassion according to the multitude of his mercies. (Lam 3:29–32)

And instead of finding multitudes of people killed by GOD in annihilation or hell torture, we find GOD and heathen reconciling:

> 11 In that day will I raise up the tabernacle of David that is fallen, and close up the breaches thereof; and I will raise up his ruins, and I will build it as in the days of old: 12 that they may possess the remnant of Edom, *and of all the heathen, which are called by my name, saith the LORD that doeth this*. 13 Behold, the days come, saith the LORD, that the plowman shall overtake the reaper, and the treader of grapes him that soweth seed; and the mountains shall drop sweet wine, and all the hills shall melt. 14 And I will bring again the captivity of my people of Israel, and they shall build the waste cities, and inhabit them; and they shall plant vineyards, and drink the wine thereof; they shall also make gardens, and eat the fruit of them. 15 And I will plant them upon their land, and they shall no more be pulled up out of their land which I have given them, saith the LORD thy God. (Amos 9:11–15)

So, death is destroyed because all people that were in hell were plucked out of it (Rev 20:13), and apparently right after that, hell and death were both destroyed (Rev 20:14). The last enemy, death, is destroyed *because all people will be at the Eschaton, and all people will be saved at that point*:

GOD (YHWH, Θεός) = Lake of Fire, Part 2

> 4 *There is one body,* and one Spirit, even as ye are called in one hope of your calling; 5 one Lord, one faith, one baptism, 6 one God and Father of all, who is above all, and through all, *and in you all.*[2] (Eph 4:4–6)

> That in the dispensation of the fulness of times he might gather together *in one all things in Christ, both which are in heaven, and which are on earth; even in him.* (Eph 1:10)

I will next explore more reasons for why Revelation 20 and 21 tell us that it is *death* that will be destroyed in the Lake of Fire, not people (condemned people), who were already removed from hell, right before hell was destroyed, and whom GOD created, loves, and saves. Look at the wording of this next passage, which leads directly into Revelation 20:14 and death and hell being cast into the Lake of Fire:

> 5 But *the rest of the dead lived not* again until the thousand years were finished. *This is the first resurrection.* 6 Blessed and holy is he that hath part in the first resurrection: on such the second death hath no power, but they shall be priests of God and of Christ, and shall reign with him a thousand years . . . 12 And I saw the dead, small and great, stand before God; and the books were opened: and another book was opened, which is the book of life: and the dead were judged out of those things which were written in the books, according to their works. 13 And the sea gave up the dead which were in it; and death and hell delivered up the dead which were in them: and they were judged *every man* according to their works. 14 And death and hell were cast into the lake of fire. This is the second death. (Rev 20:5–6; 12–14)

Verses 5 and 6 tell us that for those who take part in the first resurrection—which includes *all of the condemned*: "the rest of the dead"—death has no power over them! The first resurrection (very start of the Eschaton) is *before* the Lake of Fire (which is well into the Eschaton). This confirms that the end of death in Revelation 20:14 is just what this verse plainly says—*the death of death*—and has nothing to do with death for people (people are not mentioned in 20:14). Rather, death has ceased—it has died—and the

---

2. Some might demand that this verse is only about the church of Ephesus, but that view does not seem to be correct, since John 10:16 tells us there is one fold, as discussed heavily above, and since elsewhere in Ephesians, we are told Christ brings all things into Him (see Eph 1:10, the next verse I cite). Also, if this was only about the church of Ephesus, then this passage would contradict Col 3:11, a verse that I devote an entire chapter to below.

Hyper-Calvinist Universal Salvation

condemned are raised into salvation (1 Cor 3:12–15; 5:5; 15:52[3]) at the very start of the Eschaton, before the second death (the Lake of Fire), which refers to the death of death.

Revelation 20:5–6, 12–14 is referring to every person, such as with verse 13 referring to *the dead* as "every man." And that must be why the *next* verse is 20:14, where death and hell cease to exist, since all are being judged.[4] By the judgment, all are separated from the death and hell

---

[3]. I have cited several verses in 1 Corinthians in this book, and some of the strongest support for Hyper-Calvinist universal salvation comes from that book. But what is quite interesting is the church of Corinth was known for its horrific and blatant sexual sin (incest, etc.). Therefore, such ungodly and condemned people (1 Cor 5:5) of the church of Corinth are nevertheless saved at the Eschaton, "called to be saints" (1 Cor 1:2).

[4]. We know that the widely discussed and multifaceted concept of *judgment* in Scripture, that spans from the past (John 3:18; it likely it spans back into pre-time; see Grupp, "Why God Did Not Choose All Souls," 116, note 5), all the way to the Eschaton, involves a transformation of the dead, in varying ways, across Scripture. For example, in James 2:13, we see that GOD will judge without mercy, where that is written in a pre-Eschaton context, discussing transgression (sin). But then in Romans 11, the unbelievers have mercy from the LORD forced upon them ("yes have now obtained mercy *through their unbelief*," Rom 11:30). And the same theme continues in Rom 11:32 ("God hath concluded them all in unbelief"), via GOD's mercy (v. 31) upon *all* (v. 32). Therefore, GOD's infinite mercy can only eventually overflow and force universal salvation upon all the unbelievers and transgressors—and upon all people, who have all turned away from GOD (Rom 3:12). So, we can define GOD's judgment in terms of his *having mercy on all people*, and *transforming them* by that infinite mercy. That is what the judgment of GOD *is*, and that is why we see the following in the next two verses in Romans:

> 33 O the depth of the riches both of the wisdom and knowledge of God! how unsearchable are his judgments, and his ways past finding out! 34 For who hath known the mind of the Lord? or who hath been his counsellor? (Rom 11:33–34)

All are judged the same (2 Cor 5:10; 1 Pet 1:17), and we can define GOD's judgment as his love, mercy, and charity inevitably overtaking our lives of death and ungodliness:

> 30 And the times of this ignorance God winked at; but now commandeth all men every where to repent: 31 because he hath appointed a day, in the which he will judge the world in righteousness by that man whom he hath ordained; whereof he hath given assurance unto all men, in that he hath raised him from the dead. (Acts 17:30–31)

> 7 The way of the just is uprightness: thou, most upright, dost weigh the path of the just. 8 Yea, in the way of thy judgments, O Lord, have we waited for thee; the desire of our soul is to thy name, and to the remembrance of thee. 9 With my soul have I desired thee in the night; yea, with my spirit within me will I seek thee early: for when thy judgments are in the earth, the inhabitants of the world will learn righteousness. 10 Let favour be shewed to the wicked, yet will he not learn righteousness: in the

GOD (YHWH, Θεός) = Lake of Fire, Part 2

they were living in, in varying ways, wherein the totality of people will be transformed by being resurrected out of death and hell (Rev 20:13), for judgment, and then for preparation for the afterlife, which is the second resurrection via GOD immolation/Lake of Fire, the saving of the spirit (1 Cor 5:5), being turned into angels (Matt 11:25; Luke 20:34–36). And it is from this passage (Rev 20:5–6, 12–13) that we go directly to Revelation 20:14, where death and hell are ended, wherein only life can follow, ubiquitously, forever. And this next passage, about the commencement of the end ending of the afterlife, takes place *after* all the condemned were raised into salvation, *after* the death of death, where tears never exist again:

> And God shall wipe away all tears from their eyes; and there shall be no more death, neither sorrow, nor crying, neither shall there be any more pain: for the former things are passed away. (Rev 21:4)

The scriptural discovery that death will stop altogether, and will not exist, *after* the omnisalvation of humanity at the Eschaton, is a very important aspect of Hyper-Calvinist universal salvation, which we will use to discover and understand some of its features. That death will soon stop, after the imminent omnisalvation of humanity (Rev 20:5–6, 12–13), is what is being described in Revelation 20:14 and 1 Corinthians 15:26: hell and death cease, end, reverse, specifically by the Lake of Fire (GOD) at the Eschaton. Therefore, the people who are also thrown into the Lake of Fire at that same time during the Eschaton are thrown into a situation of *transformation: from* death *to* the death of death (from death to life), by a Baptism of Fire (Deut 5:24; Matt 3:11; Luke 3:16; Isa 13:8, the Baptism of Fire is discussed in a chapter below). Being in the Consuming Fire, GOD, who is his Innermost Fire, is about life, not death:

> 22 These words the LORD spake unto all your assembly in the mount out of the midst of the fire, of the cloud, and of the thick darkness, with a great voice: and he added no more. And he wrote them in two tables of stone, and delivered them unto me. 23 And it came to pass, when ye heard the voice out of the midst of the darkness, (for the mountain did burn with fire,) that ye came near unto me, even all the heads of your tribes, and your elders; 24 and ye said, Behold, the LORD our God hath shewed us his glory and

---

land of uprightness will he deal unjustly, and will not behold the majesty of the Lord. 11 Lord, when thy hand is lifted up, they will not see: but they shall see, and be ashamed for their envy at the people; yea, the fire of thine enemies shall devour them. (Isa 26:7–11)

his greatness, and we have heard his voice out of the midst of the fire: we have seen this day that God doth talk with man, and he liveth. 25 Now therefore why should we die? for this great fire will consume us: if we hear the voice of the LORD our God any more, then we shall die. 26 For who is there of all flesh, that hath heard the voice of the living God speaking out of the midst of the fire, as we have, and lived? (Deut 5:22–26)

So, the Lake of Fire reverses and ends death—*but that is a quality of GOD, and only GOD*. There are multiple reasons that only GOD can end death. One is because the ultimate end of human death was the reason for the cross: if Jesus, the crucified GOD (YHWH, Θεός), overcomes death, then anything that was made like him, in his image, via the incarnation, would imitate him, and therefore imitate his overcoming of death (Heb 2:17). Isaiah 25:8 can only be about the Eschaton and the future, since death has not been eliminated yet, and the verse is talking about the total elimination of death, which can only happen at the end of the world: at the point of the Lake of Fire during the Eschaton. In the future-pointing verse of Isaiah 25:8, we can see how death will be *swallowed up by (consumed by) the LORD (Consuming Fire)*, just like how *the Lake of Fire also consumes (swallows up) death* in Revelation 20:14. It seems that "consumes" and "swallows up" are identical operations, and therefore the Lake of Fire *does what GOD does*, and what only he can do: devour death. This indicates that GOD = Lake of Fire, since there is only[5] one thing that can consume and destroy death, and that is the crucified GOD. Here is the passage from Isaiah:

> 6 And in this mountain *shall* the LORD of hosts make unto all people a feast of fat things, a feast of wines on the lees, of fat things full of marrow, of wines on the lees well refined. 7 And he *will destroy* in this mountain the *face of the covering* cast over *all* people, and the vail that is spread over *all* nations. 8 He will swallow up *death in victory*; and the LORD GOD *will wipe away* tears from off *all* faces; and the rebuke of his people *shall he take away* from off all the earth: for the LORD hath spoken it. 9 And it shall be said in that day, Lo, this is our God; we have waited for him, and he *will*

---

5. According to Calvinism, and even more clearly, Hyper-Calvinism, GOD has absolute sovereignty. In a theology of maximal control by GOD (such as Hyper-Calvinism), where GOD is in control of all things, no exceptions, he would be in control of all life, *and* all death:

> See now that I, even I, am he, and there is no god with me: *I kill, and I make alive*; I wound, and I heal: neither is there any that can deliver out of my hand. (Deut 32:39)

GOD (YHWH, Θεός) = Lake of Fire, Part 2

save us: this is the Lord; we have waited for him, we *will be* glad and rejoice in his salvation. (Isa 25:6–9)

This conclusion, that GOD = Lake of Fire, should not be surprising, since GOD *is* Fire (Deut 4:24; 9:3; Heb 12:29), and since he comes in Fire at the Eschaton (2 Thess 1:7; Isa 66:15–16), where the whole world is burned up, consumed by a fire (2 Pet 3:6–7) that is so large and extensive that the heavens along with the earth will be consumed and destroyed (2 Pet 3:10–12). A fire of this extent at the end of the world would function like a massive lake or ocean of fire, *consuming* all things (bringing them to an end: the end of all things; 1 Pet 4:7). But GOD is called the *Consuming* Fire (Heb 12:29, also see Deut 4:12, 24; 5:24; Exod 3:1–6). And what is referred to as the Lake of Fire also occurs right at the Eschaton (Rev 20:11–15), consuming reality, including the dead (Rev 20:15; 21:8). And the dead are also inside the massive Eschaton Fire. We know this because if the Eschaton Fire is that extensive, then everything is inside of it, and wherever the dead are (if they are not still on earth after being cast into the Fire), they are cast into the Lake, since it is so extensive, engulfing all things. So, we know that wherever the dead are after being cast into the Lake of Fire, the dead can only coincide with the massive Eschaton Fire: the dead must be inside this Eschaton Fire (YHWH, Θεός) of 2 Peter 3. Wherever the Lake of Fire (Eschaton Fire, GOD) is located, it can only be also *collocated* with all things in its immolation, and the Lake of Fire (YHWH, Θεός) contains all of the dead, regardless of where they might be. Just as the Lake of Fire and GOD have identical key properties, so do the Lake of Fire and the Eschaton Fire. So, the descriptions of the Eschaton Fire and the Lake of Fire (GOD) are identical, and the Lake of Fire (GOD) = Eschaton Fire (GOD). The Lake of Fire = Eschaton Fire = GOD (YHWH, Θεός).

Notice, again, the future-pointing of Isaiah 25:8: "He *will* swallow up death"; "*will* wipe away tears"; "*shall* he take away." But more interestingly, notice what the *result* of swallowing up death is in verse 8: every tear is *wiped away* at the start of the afterlife (Eschaton and post-Eschaton) and right after the Lake of Fire event. We see this precise pattern at multiple places in Scripture, where immediately following the Eschaton Fire, all tears are wiped away and there is no more pain. Following Revelation 20:14, in 20:15 there is further discussion over how the dead will be thrown into the Lake of Fire (the Baptism of Fire, discussed in a chapter below), but then the next verses immediately after that, starting at Revelation 21:1, follow the same pattern as Isaiah 25:8: *death consumed (Lake of Fire)* → *no more*

Hyper-Calvinist Universal Salvation

tears. One leads right into the other. And this identical pattern is found in Isaiah 25:8–26:19: GOD consumes/swallows and therein ends death, a pattern also discussed above as being in the Parable of the Tares. Here is the passage in Revelation immediately following the death of death, where death is cast into the Lake of Fire (the second death):

> 1 And I saw *a new heaven and a new earth*: for the first heaven and the first earth *were passed away*;[6] and there was no more sea. 2 And I John saw the holy city, new Jerusalem, coming down from God out of heaven, prepared as a bride adorned for her husband. 3 And I heard a great voice out of heaven saying, Behold, the tabernacle of God is with men, and he will dwell with them, and they shall be his people, and God himself shall be with them, and be their God. 4 *And God shall wipe away all tears from their eyes*; and there shall be *no more death, neither sorrow, nor crying*, neither shall there be any more pain: for the *former things are passed away*. 5 And he that sat upon the throne said, Behold, I make *all things new*. And he said unto me, Write: for these words are true and faithful. 6 And he said unto me, It is done. I am Alpha and Omega, the beginning and the end. I will give unto him that is athirst of the fountain of the water of life freely. (Rev 21:1–6)

What we have found is that Revelation 20:14—21:6, the Parable of the Tares, and Isaiah 25:6–9 *each contain the same equation*: Lake of Fire (death consumed) ↔ no more tears/pain [afterlife]), where the arrow is meant to denote a logical biconditional, as in symbolic logic. A ↔ B: A if and only if B. There is only one thing that can conquer death, which is GOD:

> 9 who hath saved us, and called us with an holy calling, not according to our works, but according to his own purpose and grace, which was given us in Christ Jesus before the world began, 10 but is now made manifest by the appearing of our Saviour Jesus Christ, *who hath abolished death*, and hath brought life and immortality to light through the gospel ... (2 Tim 1:9–10)

> But God will redeem my soul from the power of the grave: for he shall receive me. Selah. (Ps 49:15)

> 13 The sorrows of a travailing woman shall come upon him: he is an unwise son; for he should not stay long in the place of the breaking forth of children. 14 I will ransom them from the power of the grave; I will redeem them from death: O death, I will be thy

---

6. Note that right after the Lake of Fire (Eschaton), heaven and earth are passed away, the Fire has melted and destroyed them, as discussed elsewhere in this book.

GOD (YHWH, Θεός) = Lake of Fire, Part 2

plagues; O grave, I will be thy destruction: repentance shall be hid from mine eyes. (Hos 13:13–14)

For reasons given in this chapter, these passages are considered to be discussing aspects of the same events: salvation at the Eschaton via seeing Christ as he is (at the Descension), and via immersion in Christ (immolation). And with Isaiah 25:6–9, we can see the connection of GOD swallowing up death in victory connected to Eschaton omnisalvation by its connection to the events in Isaiah 26. Isaiah 26 is a clear continuation of the account in Isaiah 25, where there is mention of devouring of enemies by fire in Isaiah 26:11. Isaiah 26 appears to contain the very specific account of Hyper-Calvinist universal salvation, where the earth casts out the dead (Isa 26:19, also see Rev 20:13), which would happen around the start of the Eschaton, and where that is right *after* the birth pangs hit a peak (Isa 26:18; also see Isa 13:8) leading into the Eschaton, and where there appears to be a reference to a hiding place, perhaps a pre-tribulation rapture scenario (Isa 26:20–21) that will be completed shortly before, and leading into, the Eschaton events (when the deliverance of the chosen is completed; see Dan 12:1–2). So, taking Isaiah 25 and 26 together reveals some of what occurs at the end of Revelation 20 and the start of Revelation 21: *death is swallowed up by, consumed by, assimilated into (digested by), the GOD (YHWH, Θεός) of infinite love and of the omnisalvation of humanity.*

Also, in Isaiah 26, note that the dead are destroyed (annihilated), where, importantly, GOD "made all their memory to perish" (verse 14), indicating that the destruction mentioned in 26:14 is specified as some sort of elimination of conscious activity (self-nonexistence), which would be in line with the discussion in a previous chapter about pre-Eschaton underworld annihilationism involving a cessation of consciousness/self. Also, in line with Jonah 2 (discussed in a chapter below), Isaiah 26:16–17 involves those entering into the annihilation (underworld consciousness cessation and/or sleep) crying out (praying) for rescue to the LORD, possibly *as they are going into consciousness cessation and/or self-nonexistence (annihilation)*. In Isaiah 26 we find this verse, which is a reference to Eschaton events:

> Thy dead men shall live, together with my dead body shall they arise. Awake and sing, ye that dwell in dust: for thy dew is as the dew of herbs, and the earth shall cast out the dead. (Isa 26:19)

Returning to our comparison of the two passages (Isa 25:6–9 and Rev 20:14—21:6) we are discussing, about GOD swallowing up and destroying

Hyper-Calvinist Universal Salvation

death, which leads directly to the end of all tears and pain via salvation by fire, we know these events—the swallowing of death in Isaiah 25:8 and in Revelation 20:14—must be the same event (the end of death), since the end of death only happens once: "The last enemy that *shall be* destroyed is death" (1 Cor 15:26). Therefore, Isaiah 25:6–9 and Revelation 20:14—21:6 are descriptions of the same event: *salvation via the Lake of Fire (GOD)*. As we are raised up, as death is about to be destroyed, ended, reversed, that is the moment "we shall be changed," when the humans who were created corrupt[7] will be made incorrupt. Consider the following passage, which also refers to the swallowing of death in victory:

> 50 Now this I say, brethren, that flesh and blood cannot inherit the kingdom of God; neither doth corruption inherit incorruption. 51 Behold, I shew you a mystery; We shall not all sleep, but we shall all be changed, 52 in a moment, in the twinkling of an eye, at the last trump: for the trumpet shall sound, and the *dead shall be raised incorruptible*, and we shall be changed. 53 For this corruptible must put on incorruption, and this mortal must put on immortality. 54 So when this corruptible shall have put on incorruption, and this mortal shall have put on immortality, then shall be brought to pass the saying that is written, *Death is swallowed up in victory*. 55 O death, where is thy sting? O grave, where is thy victory? (1 Cor 15:50–55)

Again, note the future-pointing in those two passages.[8]

---

7. This appears to be the Eschaton revelation described in 1 John 3:2. I have not seen this concept discussed previously, how humans were created as corrupt (see chapter below). It is widely assumed that humans were created in some sort of perfected or pristine (noncorrupt) state. That cannot be true, however. If GOD is the greatest of all possible beings, then he is the only that is incorrupt. This is a logical point: if there is an incorrupt entity, there can only be *one* such entity and therefore, anything that the one incorrupt creates would be *distinct* from him (lest GOD create something not distinct from himself: GOD creating more GOD). But if the one incorrupt creates something distinct from himself, it would thereby be corrupt, being *different from* the incorrupt. This is why I adhere to some sort of original sin doctrine: humans can only be created as corrupt if they are created as *distinct* from GOD. This also explains why the world is full of pain and evil (traits of incorruption): because it could only be created as *distinct* from the one who is not corrupt. And salvation of incorrupt beings appears to be as the one incorrupt (YHWH, Θεός) makes himself one with (atonement) his creatures (Gal 2:20, 1 Cor 6:17, Heb 2:11, 1 John 3:2), in varying ways and at varying times. Only what is made one with Christ (GOD) will exist.

8. Consider the following:

> And after the earthquake a fire; but the Lord was not in the fire: and after

GOD (YHWH, Θεός) = Lake of Fire, Part 2

Isaiah 25 refers to the *swallowing* of death, which would indicate a *consuming* of death, since when we swallow, or eat, we *consume*, and we assimilate what we consume. In varying ways, at varying times, humans are shown (Rom 1:20) how all is inside of GOD (Rom 11:36, 1 Cor 8:6, 2 Cor 5:18), consumed by GOD, the Consuming Fire (Heb 12:29), who is coinherently interacting with all things (Eph 1:23). Since we destroy what we eat, it would furthermore indicate that the consuming of death is a *destroying* of death: death is destroyed by the act of being eaten (consumed) and digested in GOD (Lake of Fire), bringing it into the being for absorption-assimilation. Since GOD is the *Consuming* Fire, then he is consuming all things: if he Consumes, and if he interacts with all things (such as by being their continuous Creator), then he consumes all things. That which is corrupt will be destroyed (made incorrupt), but the spirit will be changed (1 Cor 15:51, 1 John 3:2), and saved (1 Cor 5:5, 1 Cor 15:42).

There may be more to this concept of casting into the Fire than is typically noted. Consider the verses before, and leading into, Revelation 20:14:

> 7 And when the thousand years are expired, Satan shall be loosed out of his prison, 8 and shall go out to deceive the nations which are in the four quarters of the earth, Gog and Magog, to gather them together to battle: the number of whom is as the sand of the sea. 9 And they went up on *the breadth of the earth*, and compassed the camp of the saints about, and the beloved city: *and fire came down from God out of heaven, and devoured them.* (Rev 20:7–9)

---

the fire a still small voice. (1 Kgs 19:12)

This verse is not about the Eschaton Fire, as 1 Kings 19 appears to be a purely historical passage, with no recognizable references to the Eschaton events and the Eschaton Fire. The fire referenced in verse 19 appears to be a natural event, such as a forest fire or the like, as the fire is mentioned at the end of a string of natural events (wind, earthquake, then fire), all of which GOD was not inside of. So, 1 Kings 19 would not be a passage that is both an historical account, but also a foretelling of the Eschaton—as many passages of Scripture involve that sort of two-fold approach.

There is the additional question of how the omnipresent GOD *cannot be at some place*, such as "in the fire," referenced in 1 Kgs 19:12. It is impossible that the omnipresent GOD could not be at some location. For this reason, I can only conclude that what 1 Kings 19 is referring to is the incarnated GOD (Christ, the Word made flesh), since Christ, though he was/is GOD, can be considered to be at location A and not at location B), since he is confined to being in a physical body, such as a human body, as is the case in our particular cosmos, and which can only be at its finite location in space. In verse 11, it says, "the LORD passed by," being another reference to GOD as incarnated, moving about like a spirit, an angel, and/or a human.

Hyper-Calvinist Universal Salvation

We see in this passage, which is in the context of the Lake of Fire, that there is Fire that comes to earth, when all the nations, and all the earth ("the breadth of the earth"), will be *devoured* in Fire from, and of, *GOD*. So, in this passage, the Eschaton event is a *devouring/consuming*. But this Eschaton event also involves things being *thrown into* the Fire. So, the Fire of the Eschaton (YHWH, Θεός) both goes to things and devours them, but this same Fire also has things going to it and into it. The Fire both goes to things and things go to it, in seeming opposite directions of activity. But since GOD is everywhere, how can things go in and out of GOD? I think the answer is that they cannot, since nothing can be ever outside of GOD.[9] So, these motions, of things going to the Fire, and the Fire going to things, must involve a non-spatiotemporal sort of interaction with GOD, a non-spatiotemporal sort of being with GOD. But "cast into" nevertheless involves spatiotemporal conceptualization, and consuming and devouring do also, such as of items moving through space and time, and changing through space and time. So, some sort of change must be going on, including changes of location, of *some* sort, in this devouring and casting into the Lake of Fire. If the casting into the Fire and being devoured by the Fire are not describable via ordinary spatiotemporal concepts, since GOD is everywhere and we cannot move in and out of him, then what other sort of change must be going on, which is being described in the casting of death, hell, and people into the Lake of Fire?

An answer to this question is, it seems, easy to come to, being found right in the verses we just referred to (1 Cor 15:42, for example). He is in all things ("all in all," Eph 1:23) and, coinherently, all things are inside the omnipresent creator-GOD, where, strictly speaking, something cannot go, for example, *from outside of him to inside of him*,[10] as it might be imagined

---

9. In the KJV, there are a few verses about people being separated from GOD, such as Isa 59:2; Jer 5:8; Ezek 14:5; and most notably 2 Thess 1:9. These verses seems to be either about a human consciousness, that is distracted from the LORD, or one that has gone into self-nonexistence until the Eschaton, as with 2 Thess 1:9.

10. In thinking over this topic of coinherence through the years, I have found it difficult to distinguish the concept that *GOD is in all things*, on the one hand, from the supposedly opposite concept of how *all things are in GOD*, on the other. If GOD is *all in all* (Eph 1:23, KJV wording), this seems to likewise blur the lines between these two concepts, if you digest the concepts within the words, "He is all in all." If we break apart that philosophically *rich* phrase, it has (at least) two concepts within it: he is all, and he is in all, which are the two scenarios we are considering in this footnote: GOD *is in all*, and *all is* GOD. Regarding the concept that *he is all*, I want to introduce the idea that "he is all" is a concept that should be housed within the undeveloped, but ecstatic, theology

GOD (YHWH, Θεός) = Lake of Fire, Part 2

is happening in Revelation 20:14. The "casting" of Revelation 20:14 is not a from *here to there*, spatiotemporally, but rather, must be from being one way, to being another: a quality or state change, for lack of better words, rather than a spatiotemporal location change. And specifically, a change we find referenced in the context of the Eschaton verses, which is about at least one aspect of the change humans undergo at the Eschaton, is from corrupted to incorrupt. And this change from corruption to incorruption happens via alterations in, and dramatic escalations of, *GOD's revelation*, where he, as infinite Fire, is revealed as Fire, directly seen and experienced fully in his Being, as infinite, supernatural Fire (YHWH, Θεός)—Fire that is Spirit (John 4:24)—therein impacting, transforming, burning the person in a way that previously was not yet happening, bringing the person from one state of revelation (pre-Fire-revealing, pre-Eschaton) to another state of revelation (seeing GOD's Fire directly, fully, as he is [1 John 3:2], at the

---

of *Hyper-Calvinism*, within which, the proper perspective would be that GOD has such sovereignty, that it's hard to not find GOD everywhere one looks; he is finally, truly acknowledged in all things (Prov 3:5–6), as the one who constantly, moment-to-moment, is producing all aspects of this production of reality, we are all prisoners within (Zech 9:11; Ps 79:11; Phlm 1:1). In this production, he moves the atoms, and brings forth and moves all the love, and violence, and stillness, and creativity glutting this physical reality we temporarily are living in. This totalist sovereignty (hyper-sovereignty) of GOD, which I want to claim should be considered an aspect of the important theology of Hyper-Calvinism, is GOD's perfect way (2 Sam 22:31), perfect production, *of his love*, in saving the world (John 3:17) and restoring all things (Acts 3:21). So, by this, we know he *is all* (also see Col 3:11). But additionally, "He is all in all" contains the concept that he is *in* all. If one conceptualizes the totalist omnipresence that GOD has with whatever he creates, which is everything (Rev 4:11), I find that the concept that GOD is most deeply *in all things, collapses*, in my mind, into the supposedly opposite scenario of *all things in GOD*. If GOD is in all things, and as deeply as possible (presumably in ways we can't even understand, as Eph 1:23 implies), inside every atom, every mind, every bit of energy, every universe, thought, every dimension, every empty void (for lack of better words), every butterfly and sand grain, in every way, then GOD would be describable as something like an ultra-massive, ultra deep ocean of his Being, for lack of better words, which *everything* is submerged within (consumed by) and maximally penetrated by, that we are all moving through (Acts 17:28) each day. But that sounds just like we are saying, all things *are in* GOD. So, these concepts—GOD is in all things, and all things are in GOD—appear to collapse into each other, and break-down into each other. He is in us, and we are in him (John 15:5); this is called coinherence. And likewise, the concept of GOD *devouring* all things, versus things being *cast into* him, might be descriptions of the same events at the Eschaton. And finally, but most importantly, the aforementioned totalist sovereignty of GOD we are discussing, in the Hyper-Calvinist theology of GOD's hyper-sovereignty (another way of saying true sovereignty), leads to *fear of GOD*—inner fear of GOD, the beginning of wisdom (Prov 9:10)—in understanding the true power and transcendence of all that is unfolding in this physical reality from moment to moment.

Eschaton). This is why GOD is referred to as "revealed," in a revealing event that will end all things at the end of the world:

> And to you who are troubled rest with us, when the Lord Jesus *shall be revealed* from heaven with his mighty angels. (2 Thess 1:7)

> Beloved, now are we the sons of God, and it doth not yet appear what we shall be: but we know that, when he shall appear, we shall be like him; for we shall see him as he is. (1 John 3:2)

When GOD is revealed at the Eschaton, where all see him together, every person will see him as omnipresent Spirit Fire. Everything will realize, experience, feel, and know him, the Consuming Fire, the Lake of Fire, the crucified GOD.

The Fire is already here, of course, but not revealed yet (at least not to human beings, at this point in time, except for individual instances here and there—Damascus Road, the martyrdom of Stephen, Francis of Assisi's seraphic stigmata, the martyrdom of Saint Laurentian [Saint Lawrence], to give a few examples). The coming Eschaton shift of revelation is the change from being *one* way to *another*, by our awareness and seeing of the Eschaton Fire at the end of all things, is what is being described in Scripture. Revelation 20 (and Isaiah 25–26) points toward the casting into the Lake of Fire as being GOD's immolation of the heavens and the earth. GOD's Fire will arrive quickly, and bring everything into destruction, into the second death and the second resurrection—both of which *are the Lake of Fire*:

> But the day of the Lord will come as a thief in the night; in the which the heavens shall pass away with a great noise, and the elements shall melt with fervent heat, the earth also and the works that are therein shall be burned up. (2 Pet 3:10)

The casting into the Lake of Fire is the unveiling of GOD and his Consuming Fire.

Continuing on in Revelation 20, next we have the following passage:

> 9 And they went up on the breadth of the earth, and compassed the camp of the saints about, and the beloved city: and fire came down from God out of heaven, and devoured them. 10 And the devil that deceived them was cast into the *lake of fire* and brimstone, where the beast and the false prophet are, and shall be tormented day and night for ever and ever. 11 And I saw a great white throne, and him that sat on it, from whose face the earth and the heaven fled away; and there was found no place for them. 12 And I saw

GOD (YHWH, Θεός) = Lake of Fire, Part 2

> the dead, small and great, stand before God; and the books were opened: and another book was opened, which is the book of life: and the dead were judged out of those things which were written in the books, according to their works. 13 And the sea gave up the dead which were in it; and death and hell delivered up the dead which were in them: and they were judged every man according to their works. (Rev 20:9-13)

Verse 9 discusses how there is fire from GOD, to devour the whole earth, where this moves directly into discussing the Lake of Fire in verse 10, as if the two are the same fire. Is the fire of verses 7-9 the same as that of verse 10-14 (Lake of Fire)? In verse 11, we find that the earth is still intact, since people could still run away from GOD. So, Revelation 20:7-14 cannot involve a chronological account that is unfolding, and instead it appears to involve a list of events, jumping from topic to topic, talking about what is about to happen, which is how the earth will be destroyed by the Fire of GOD at the end of the age. That would include the dead of the earth and inside the earth, just as the Lake of Fire has the dead put into it at the end of the age: both the fire of verses 7-9 and of the Lake of Fire of verses 10 and on into chapter 21 are massive fires that have the dead of the earth in them. And there is no mention that the Lake of Fire is some other location, other than earth; its location is not mentioned, and it merely follows form the fire of verses 7-9, which cover all of the earth. Furthermore, verse 9 tells us that the fire is *of GOD*, and we know that the Lake of Fire is doing what only GOD can do (end death), so it seems difficult to avoid asserting that the fire of Revelation 20:7-9 is anything but *identical* to the Lake of Fire of Revelation 20:10-14 and into chapter 21. And if that is the case, then the fire that consumes the "breadth of the earth" at the Eschaton is none other than GOD's direct Spirit-presence, GOD's full revealing. The fire that consumes (Consuming Fire, YHWH, Θεός) is the Lake of Fire (GOD), and people are cast into him because *he arrives* not from another place, but he arrives in our awareness, when he is *revealed*, to immolate people, and put their minds into amazement:

> 6 Howl ye; for the day of the Lord is at hand; it shall come as a destruction from the Almighty. 7 Therefore shall all hands be faint, and every man's heart shall melt: 8 and they shall be afraid: pangs and sorrows shall take hold of them; they shall be in pain as a woman that travaileth: they shall be amazed one at another; their faces shall be as flames. (Isa 13:6-8)

Hyper-Calvinist Universal Salvation

A fire is not usually thought of as being a liquid, but rather as a plasma state of matter. So, the Lake of Fire, the Fire of GOD's Being, must not be like ordinary, earthly fire—like the fire of a forest fire—that we are familiar with from this physical reality. Also, and importantly, when something goes into a lake, it is immersed by the lake, surrounded by the lake; in other words, it is as if the lake swallows and consumes that which is *in* it (*inside of* it). And Revelation 20:14 does involve the going into the Lake: death and hell are cast *into* the Lake of Fire: the aforementioned shift of how GOD reveals himself to humans and to creation. The Greek for "into" is εἰς, which can represent the penetration *of a union*. I find this quite revealing, in that it indicates the oneness with, and union with, GOD humans are given fully at the Eschaton. εἰς would mean that the casting into the Lake of Fire of Revelation 20:14 surrounds, consumes, the people that go into it, and which goes into them, where in this being swallowed, like Isaiah 25:8, that which is swallowed enters, penetrates, into the being of that which swallows it, and is assimilated into that which swallows it, as in a process of digestion. Herein is the supernatural coinherence of the omnipresent and omnicausal GOD (the crucified GOD) in relationship of infinite love to all of his creation, and, I propose, to all things, all of which is groaning for his return (his revealing), "waiting for the adoption, to wit, the redemption of our body" (Rom 8:23).

Going back to 1 Corinthians 15, where death is again referred to as being "swallowed up," indicating that the reference in 1 Corinthians 15 is to the Lake of Fire (GOD), the Eschaton Fire, in 1 Corinthians 15:52 *the dead*, the sleeping, which are the condemned, the unchosen, are *raised uncorrupted*. Through the Fire (which starts with the Descension) comes a transformation, comes salvation: from corruption into noncorruption, indicating how this Eschaton Fire is a restoring (Acts 3:21; Col 1:20; 1 Cor 3:12–15). This is Hyper-Calvinist universal salvation, where residents of the Lake of Fire are burned and saved in the Eschaton, as hell (or Hades) and death are ended by being consumed by, and cast into, GOD.

> 42 So also is the resurrection of the dead. It is sown in corruption; it is raised in incorruption: 43 it is sown in dishonour; it is raised in glory: it is sown in weakness; it is raised in power: 44 *it is sown a natural body; it is raised a spiritual body*. There is a natural body, and there is a spiritual body. (1 Cor 15:42–44)

If the dead are raised in incorruption (this is the second resurrection, see below), then they are saved, and there are no dead (universal salvation).

GOD (YHWH, Θεός) = Lake of Fire, Part 2

This passage is not about a particular group of the dead, but rather, it is about *the dead, in general*—that is, about *all* the dead.

> Thou *shalt* make them as a fiery oven in the time of thine anger: the Lord *shall swallow* them up in his wrath, and the fire *shall devour* them. (Ps 21:9)

This illuminating verse about the Eschaton encompasses much of what we have discussed in this chapter. The people are made into an oven, as if transformed, set on fire (Isa 13:8), because there is suddenly Fire everywhere. And this passage is about the condemned, I believe, since it is a verse about the *wrath* of GOD at the Eschaton. The message is that the condemned are suddenly in the omnipresent Lake of Fire, swallowed up, assimilating into GOD.

In Psalm 21:9, the reference to the fiery oven is the swallowing/consuming event of the Eschaton Fire (GOD). We will see other references in this book about the fiery oven or furnace, which we have reason to believe are references to the Lake of Fire of the Eschaton of GOD that raises all dead, and saves all. The condemned are made for this day (Eschaton):

> The Lord hath made all things for himself: yea, even the wicked for the day of evil. (Prov 16:4)

First John 3:2 tells us the condemned (and the salvific) are their true selves on that day, and for that reason, that day (the Eschaton) is what humanity was created for, made possible by humanity's crucified GOD (Christ, Consuming Fire, YHWH, Θεός). Those who were predestined to die *are preserved*:

> Let the sighing of the prisoner come before thee; according to the greatness of thy power preserve thou those that are appointed to die ... (Ps 79:11)

13

The Twinkling of the Eye Is before the Earth Is Destroyed by Fire (Lake of Fire)

THE VERSES IMMEDIATELY FOLLOWING the death of death in Revelation 20:14–15 are about the new heaven and earth:

> 1 And I saw a new heaven and a new earth: for the first heaven and the first earth were passed away; and there was no more sea. 2 And I John saw the holy city, new Jerusalem, coming down from God out of heaven, prepared as a bride adorned for her husband. 3 And I heard a great voice out of heaven saying, Behold, the tabernacle of God is with men, and he will dwell with them, and they shall be his people, and God himself shall be with them, and be their God. (Rev 21:1–3)

As discussed in a chapter above, and putting the matter in different words, an error of the popular view is to claim that Revelation 20:14 is *not* about the death of death, but rather is about the death *of souls*—and specifically condemned souls—where the Lake is actually GOD's hell torture, annihilating or torturing humans forever, where *that* is the second death. But how can that be what Revelation 20:14 is saying? It is hard to imagine how any such misunderstanding could have ever developed in the pop theology, which includes the popular and traditional view of hell, since all who were in hell were removed from it the verse prior (Rev 20:13), so how could souls then die in hell after that, such as when hell was destroyed in the next verse in the KJV wording ("Hades," in the newer translations)? If Revelation 20:14 were about souls dying, the verse would read something like this: "unsaved souls were cast into the Lake of Fire, this is the second death." But Revelation 20:14 is saying something quite different. It has no mention of people, souls, or any living beings of any sort whatsoever that are cast into the Lake of Fire, and there is no mention of any sort of hell-like qualities to the Lake of Fire. Rather, Revelation 20:14 says that *death itself* will be cast into the Lake of Fire: death has *died*. And it seems safe to say that this means that death, at the Eschaton, will be stopped, and therefore reversed, ended. So, all death will cease by the Lake of Fire. The exact term "lake of fire" is used late in the book of Revelation at the time of the Eschaton. If the Lake of Fire were identical to hell and/or Hades, as is the case with the erroneous popular view of hell, then Revelation 20:14 would amount to maintaining that the Lake of Fire is thrown into the Lake of Fire (or hell was thrown into hell), which is nonsensical.

A key point is that, after this, those who were removed from hell, right before hell was destroyed, are then, after hell no longer exists (after it dies, along with death dying), put into the Lake of Fire. They are removed from hell (Rev 20:13), hell and Hades are destroyed, and death is destroyed (Rev 20:14), and then the sinners who were removed from hell are put into a different Fire (which can't be hell since hell no longer exists), which is the Fire of Christ (GOD). Consider the following verses:

> *And* whosoever was not found written in the book of life was cast into the lake of fire. (Rev 20:15)

> But the fearful, and unbelieving, and the abominable, and murderers, and whoremongers, and sorcerers, and idolaters, and all liars, shall have their part in the lake which burneth with fire and brimstone: which is the second death. (Rev 21:8)

The first death is condemnation and body death, and the second death is the death of death, as we saw above. But it is apparently after all of this is finished, that the aforementioned are put into the Lake of Fire. But there is no third death, since death no longer exists, and thus the Lake of Fire can only be of life, not death. In Revelation 20:14, we find that with this second death, death dies, and hell dies, but then at the start of Revelation 20:15 is the word "And," indicating a new concept therefore starts, but where there is continuation of thought from the previous verse. This "And" brings the connection between verse 14 and verse 15, as if to say: *in addition to* death and hell dying in the Lake of Fire, *also* sinners are put into the Lake of Fire during this time, all of which is the second death: death and hell being ended in GOD (Fire), and sinners being thrown into that same GOD-Fire—but there is no mention of death or termination of the sinners by this Fire, but rather, only their salvation (1 Cor 3:12–15, Luke 3:16). This is roughly repeated in Revelation 21:8. So, *which is it*: are the unchosen put in the Lake to *also* die (Rev 20:15; 21:8), or it is *just* that death dies (20:14), as argued above, where the unchosen, being *also* in the Fire, have some *other* function in being there? It would appear that the answer is in the very wording of the KJV text: there is no death, since it has ceased, and thus the persons in the Lake of Fire cannot be affected by death, and have some other function in being in the Lake of Fire (YHWH, Θεός). All people (all selves, all consciousnesses, all souls that house self and consciousness) are *in a state of resurrection* (the first resurrection) by the time of the Lake of Fire, and I do not know of any Scripture that indicates *anything* like the following (which would be needed if one is to claim that the first resurrection is reversed and the resurrected are again killed by GOD a second time during the Eschaton): those *just* resurrected who are in GOD's Fire (Lake of Fire), who were resurrected for the first time at the very start of the Eschaton, are nevertheless annihilated and/or tortured in hell. We do not see that in Scripture, and instead we see only commentary about death dying—not humans, who all are saved, and thus cannot be anything but made one with Christ (YHWH, Θεός). Revelation 20:14 *defines* the second death as the death of death and hell, and no scripture discusses people being of this second death, and for that reason, the second death is the death of death, *and* the universal salvation and GOD-immolation of all condemned souls.

Also, and very important to our discussion in this chapter and the previous chapter, it appears that the Bible is telling us that death is swallowed up *before* the nonsalvific are cast into the Lake of Fire (GOD) to be saved (see below). This would conclusively indicate that those in the Lake of Fire are *not* in it for destruction (permanent self-nonexistence in a second annihilation) or conscious torment (traditional view of hell), but just the opposite: for being prepared for, transformed for, the afterlife. This is the aforementioned other function that the condemned (and any of the salvific that are in the Lake) have in the Lake of Fire (Eschaton Fire). We know this because 1 Corinthians 15:54 tells us that death is destroyed *at the last trumpet* (1 Thess 4:16–17, cited below), which is at the very start of the Eschaton, and thus clearly before the omnipresent Lake of Fire commences on and in the earth. We know that the Eschaton starts before the last trumpet, so the Eschaton has events before the last trumpet.

> 14 For if we believe that Jesus died and rose again, even so them also which sleep in Jesus will God bring with him. 15 For this we

say unto you by the word of the Lord, that we which are alive and remain unto the coming of the Lord shall not prevent them which are asleep. 16 For the Lord himself shall descend from heaven with a shout, with the voice of the archangel, and with the *trump of God*: and the dead in Christ shall rise first: 17 then we which are alive and remain shall be caught up together with them in the clouds, to meet the Lord in the air: and so shall we ever be with the Lord. 18 Wherefore comfort one another with these words. (1 Thess 4:14–18)

Note that this does not refer to this trump at GOD's descending to earth to meet us in the clouds as being the *last* trump. And there is no mention of death being swallowed up in victory yet. Verses 16 and 17 seem to include *all* people, and it says in verse 16 that the dead are "dead in Christ." The word for "in" is the Greek ἐν, often related to pregnancy, where one person is inside another (such as ἐν in Matt 1:18; 2:1), or when an object existing in its location or area. Therefore, after the first death and pre-Eschaton annihilation, the dead (unsaved) are already considered as inside the omnipresent GOD. So, they are not burned yet, but they are awakened into self-existence in GOD, but they are still not, strictly speaking, saved and given salvation. Consider:

> 25 Verily, verily, I say unto you, The hour is coming, and now is, when the dead shall hear the voice of the Son of God: *and they that hear shall live.* 26 For as the Father hath life in himself; so hath he given to the Son to have life in himself; 27 and hath given him authority to execute judgment also, because he is the Son of man. 28 Marvel not at this: for the hour is coming, in the which all that are in the graves shall hear his voice, 29 and shall come forth; they that have done good, unto the resurrection of life; and they that have done evil, *unto the resurrection of damnation.* (John 5:25–29)

14

Two Resurrections at Each End of the Thousand Years in a Day

SO, THE *DEAD* HEAR GOD's voice while still in the grave (verses 25 and 28), but they are not yet saved, and they *resurrect into damnation*: still in the corrupted state, at the early and first parts of the Eschaton (at the last trump), and after being resurrected from the pre-Eschaton annihilation. So we do not have reason to believe this passage in 1 Thessalonians 4, just cited near the end of the last chapter, is talking about the same precise time and event as the death of death in the Eschaton Fire of GOD, the Lake of Fire, which reaches full intensity at a later point in the Eschaton.

And the following passage reveals to us the sequence of events:

> 51 Behold, I shew you a mystery; We shall not all sleep, but we shall *all* be changed, 52 in a moment, in the twinkling of an eye, *at the last trump*: for the trumpet shall sound, *and the dead shall be raised incorruptible*, and we shall be changed. 53 For this corruptible must put on incorruption, and this mortal must put on immortality. 54 So when this corruptible shall have put on incorruption, and this mortal shall have put on immortality, *then* shall be brought to pass the saying that is written, *Death is swallowed up in victory*. (1 Cor 15:51–54)

This verifies that the dead are not eliminated or tortured at the Fire Eschaton (Lake of Fire). In John 5:28–29 the dead are raised damned, but in 1 Corinthians 15:54 the dead are raised incorruptible. So, *there are (at least) two clear stages of sequential events in the Eschaton.*

There is a question of the apparent separation in time of (1) the lifting up (that is, rapturing—but see below, the scriptural account of the

Two Resurrections at Each End of the Thousand Years in a Day

rapturing of the chosen is not in line with the pop theology about of a pre-trib rapture) of the salvific to Christ in a place above (in the clouds, 1 Thess 4:16–18), then (2) *later, in fact one thousand years later*, the condemned are resurrected (the "first resurrection"). Revelation 20:4–6 involves a span of time, en epoch (perhaps from the cross to the start of the thousand years) of the chosen being raised, or raptured, but, *importantly*, the chosen are all raised *before* the millennial kingdom happens (this lifting, or rapturing, of GOD's chosen is apparently completed by the very start of the thousand years in a day, with an apparently surging of this activity nearer to the Eschaton start, and specifically at the start of the thousand years in a day, see Dan 11:45-12:3). This is also indicated in Revelation 20:6, which tells us the chosen, and specifically those martyred for not taking the mark of the beast (see Rev 20:4), will reign with Christ for *all* of the thousand years, and thus will be lifted up at least by the start of the thousand years. There are the chosen, who are taken-up by the LORD, from, it appears, the time of the cross to the time of the mark of the beast. This is roughly a rapture concept, or what is called the deliverance in Dan 12:1-2 (KJV wording), where during that time, when the chosen die (in their physical bodies), and the LORD meets them in the clouds. This seems similar the martyrdom of Stephen at the end of Acts 7, where when Stephen meets the LORD before going into annihilation sleep, he meets the LORD at the clouds: the LORD Is at the clouds, which is, it seems, where he meets the elect at the time of body death, regardless if the person is raptured into the place of hiding during the time of the wrath. So, there are two events we are referring to: (1) the lifting up of the chosen, then one thousand years later is (2) the resurrection of the unchosen-condemned (the "first resurrection" of Rev 20:5). The lifting up, or rapturing, of the chosen to a place above is completed at the Descension of GOD (Christ) *from* heaven *to* the clouds, apparently during the time of the early implementation of the mark of the beast (see below), wherein the salvific are raised and taken up (1 Thess 4:16–17), *before the thousand years starts*. And then the Lake of Fire Baptism is *after* the thousand years (Rev 20:5), and thus we have clear indication that the rapturing of the chosen and the resurrecting of the unchosen of the first resurrection *are separated by the thousand years*. So, the chosen reside in a waiting place, often referred to by the perhaps-misleading name "intermediate state."

There are a decent number of these passages that discuss a situation that appears to involve the chosen/salvific being lifted to a beautiful waiting place (Isa 25:6–8, for example), directly with GOD, waiting in the clouds,

Hyper-Calvinist Universal Salvation

in the mountains above the mountains (see Isa 2:2–3; Matt 24:31—many passages discuss this, especially in Isaiah and the Minor Prophets), waiting out the time, perhaps a few years long, of the wrath at the very end of time (see also Isa 26:15–21), leading directly into the Eschaton. The lifting of the chosen has to be *completed* near the Eschaton in time, and in the time of the very end, with the last of them lifted up as the mark of the beast is being forced onto all people (Rev 13:16). We know this by Revelation 20:4, where we are told that those who reject the mark *reigned with Christ for the thousand years*. So, the thousand years do not *start* until into the time of the mark (and we know the mark, whatever it is, has not started, in our present day, yet), and which is in the very last handful of years, the time of the great tribulation. So, the thousand years is during the last year or short time before the Eschaton. So, we have a situation where *a thousand years is in just a year or a few years—how can this be?*

I believe the answer to that, and the way to make sense of this situation, is plainly stated in Scripture, if we look to the following and enormously underdiscussed passage in 2 Peter:

> 7 but the heavens and the earth, which are now, by the same word are kept in store, reserved unto fire against the day of judgment and perdition of ungodly men. 8 But, beloved, be not ignorant of this one thing, that one day is with the Lord as a thousand years, and a thousand years as one day. (2 Pet 3:7–8)

Notice that this passage is specifically altering the normal concepts of chronologically experienced time and any ordinary philosophy of time, in multiple ways, such as in smearing together the Eschaton Fire with time *before* the Eschaton, as if the Fire of the end is experienced now (a concept discussed elsewhere in Scripture, and in this book). And more significantly, verse 8 is providing us with a very new and different philosophy of time, and what could seemingly be considered a *coinherently fractal philosophy of time*, where a thousand years and one day are somehow nested *within* each other. This is difficult for humans to understand, but probably much more like GOD's way of creating and experiencing time. But since this passage is in the context of the very chronological *end* of all things, including discussion of the LORD as a thief in the night (2 Pet 3:10), for example, it seems best to interpret 2 Peter 3:8 *as referring primarily to the last years of earth leading into the Eschaton*. I understand that this is a very different view than is usually discussed in the post- and pre-millennial theologies, but I believe those do not utilize or take into account a Hyper-Calvinist hyper-literal

Two Resurrections at Each End of the Thousand Years in a Day

reading of 2 Peter 3:8, and a reading of it in its context, where doing so allows us to bring into an improved understanding the thousand years (which is *both* one thousand years *and* just a short time, as just mentioned), which, as we will discuss, roughly coincide with the Great Tribulation, and may involve some sort of alternate reality, and time-bending reality. Typically, those discussing eschatology will refer to the great tribulation as seven years (which, contrary to popular opinion, is *not* a straightforward concept to extract from Scripture), ignoring 2 Peter 3:8. That is in conflict to what has just been written.

There is enormous disagreement and confusion in the theologies of the millennium, and again, I believe because they ignore 2 Peter 3:8's reference to a new philosophy of time that happens from the time of the mark of the beast and into the start of the Eschaton, as the scriptures we just cited above reveal. The amount of discrepancy amongst dispensational premillennialists, historic premillennialists, postmillennialists, and amillennialists should tip us off to something missing in these theologies, and thus to perhaps look to the alternative theory of time just proposed: the coming coinherent fractal time that enters the scene from the mark of the beast to the first resurrection (see Rev 20:5, referring to the condemned raised at the start of the Eschaton, at the end of the thousand years).

There are many references in Scripture as to a quite altered reality coming into greater and greater visibility during the time at the very end, such as dead people walking around (Ezek 37; Isa 26:18–20; also see Matt 27:52), unicorns descending to earth (Isa 34:7 KJV wording), the sun and moon greatly brightening (Isa 30:26; Rev 16:8) and then going dark (Rev 6:12), seas and rivers drying up (Isa 19:5–6), a one-world religion (Dan 11:36-37; 2 Thess 2:4), where people are forced to take a mark in their bodies to buy and sell (Rev 13:15–18), stars falling to the ground (right before the sky rolls up; see Rev 6:13–14)—there are many events from Scripture that could be listed. And Scripture contains multiple references to what best could be called a fractal coinherence of events, time, and space. For example, Christ is All in all (Eph 1:23, KJV WORDING): he is the All that is in all things. Reality, the Totality (GOD and all things he's created), is an omnipresently coinhering (omni-coinhering) infinite hyperspace between GOD and the creations of GOD, where everything is totally opened and exposed directly to him in every way, eternally (see Heb 4:13). We are in Christ and he in us (John 15:5). And notably, there are references to the time of the "Antichrist" in the last few years as being of a different sort

Hyper-Calvinist Universal Salvation

of time and existence than we are familiar with in ordinary life, which is referenced three times in Revelation 17, such as "the beast that was, and is not, and yet is" (verse 8)—wow! Something very different is going on in this physical reality at the final years of the aforementioned fractal coinherent time (for lack of better words). Note how that verse from Revelation 17 contains what appears to be a blatant contradiction ("is not and yet is"), much like the thousand years being one year, and vice versa. Some of those who are alive in that time (after all rapturing is completed, and the Descension revealing has at least started, in some way, and the thousand years has started) will have what these verses entail revealed to them, but I do not believe we can understand them until we see this upcoming and imminent reality, of thousand year years, and entities that are not and yet are. Approaching the Eschaton, there is a bit of Scripture supporting the idea of some sort of time-warping hyperreality replacing ordinary reality, from the mark to the Eschaton (the thousand years). Note that in this model of the end times, which comes from the Hyper-Calvinist hyper-literalist approach to Scripture, the Eschaton in full revealing does not start at the exact same time for all people, and further it starts for the chosen before it does for the unchosen.

Using much of the Scripture cited in this book so far, and using Revelation 20:4–6 and 1 Thessalonians 4:16–17, the following timeline of the Eschaton can be constructed from the hyper-literalist reading of Scripture that Hyper-Calvinist universal salvation involves:

1. First death: original sin, all falling short, and body death, into annihilation (temporary pre-Eschaton self-nonexistence).
2. Resurrection of the dead in Christ (epoch of delivering, rapturing, GOD's chosen).
3. Descension of Christ (GOD): the full, total revealing of Christ, at the last trump and the first resurrection, the chosen change in an instant, with GOD in a waiting space in the sky, or in the mountains above the mountains.
4. The thousand years (in a day), the time of the alternate, and possibly hypnagogic, hyperreality.
5. The rest of the dead are raised (*after* the thousand years; see Rev 20:5).
6. Final rapture, including for those still on earth.

7. Second death (has two aspect to it): Lake of Fire: (a) death of hell, and the death of death, and (b) the burning away of the corruption of sinners in order to save them via GOD-immolation.

The unsaved are saved by Fire (1 Cor 3:15), so GOD must be revealed as Fire at step 2, where all flesh sees him together by somewhere between points 6 and 7. And surely most, if it's not the case that all, will be burned by GOD (Lake of Fire) at that point, but what is very important to note is how much happens before the Lake of Fire (apparently the most intense GOD revealing). The Descension, and seeing GOD has he is (1 John 3:2) is an event of GOD's Fire revelation of the Eschaton, but that initial fiery descending and revealing is perhaps in some way distinct from, or not as intense as the even more intense full-on Lake of Fire, the second death. The following passage, which is one of the many that were engineered by GOD in Scripture where historic events are, and were, fractals of the coming Eschaton events, is a passage that may give scriptural evidence for this initial fieriness of the Eschaton, before the full immolation of the Lake of GOD (Lake of Fire):

> 14 And when ye see this, your heart shall rejoice, and your bones shall flourish like an herb: and the hand of the LORD shall be known toward his servants, and his indignation toward his enemies. 15 For, behold, the LORD will come with fire, and with his chariots like a whirlwind, to render his anger with fury, and his rebuke with flames of fire. 16 For by fire and by his sword will the LORD plead with all flesh: and the slain of the LORD shall be many. 17 They that sanctify themselves, and purify themselves in the gardens behind one tree in the midst, eating swine's flesh, and the abomination, and the mouse, shall be consumed together, saith the LORD. 18 For I know their works and their thoughts: it shall come, that I will gather all nations and tongues; and they shall come, and see my glory. 19 And I will set a sign among them, and I will send those that escape of them unto the nations, to Tarshish, Pul, and Lud, that draw the bow, to Tubal, and Javan, to the isles afar off, that have not heard my fame, neither have seen my glory; and they shall declare my glory among the Gentiles. 20 And they shall bring all your brethren for an offering unto the LORD out of all nations upon horses, and in chariots, and in litters, and upon mules, and upon swift beasts, to my holy mountain Jerusalem, saith the LORD, as the children of Israel bring an offering in a clean vessel into the house of the LORD. 21 And I will also take of them for priests and for Levites, saith the LORD. 22 For as the new

Hyper-Calvinist Universal Salvation

> heavens and the new earth, which I will make, shall remain before me, saith the LORD, so shall your seed and your name remain. 23 And it shall come to pass, that from one new moon to another, and from one sabbath to another, shall all flesh come to worship before me, saith the Lord. 24 And they shall go forth, and look upon the carcases of the men that have transgressed against me: for their worm shall not die, neither shall their fire be quenched; and they shall be an abhorring unto all flesh. (Isa 66:14–24)

We know that this passage has part of its context in the Eschaton events, since it starts off saying that the bones shall flourish *like* plant life (not equal to it, but like it), resembling the bones that live in Ezekiel 37. In this passage from Isaiah 66, we can see a lot of fiery activities going on right when the LORD arrives (descends), but the activities of a passage like this indicate that full immolation, immersion in the Lake of GOD, has not been revealed yet. He is Fire when he arrives (Isa 66:15), interacting with humanity as Fire (66:16). All will be consumed (66:17), after all nations are gathered to see him (66:18) together (this may be a reference to the thousand years: the thousand years in a day), where this may take place over a calendar month-long period (66:23). This means that GOD is not most fully revealed as Fire at the early stages of the Eschaton, and as he will be in his full intensity at the Lake of Fire event, where all is destroyed by Fire, bringing the end of all things (1 Pet 4:7).

What is perhaps most important about this, for understanding Hyper-Calvinist universal salvation, is that this precise breakdown of the Eschaton events reveals that the last trump (when the chosen are changed in the twinkling) is *before* the thousand years (or at the very start of it), and, *ipso facto*, before the Lake of Fire. And salvation for them is *before* those of Revelation 20–21 are cast into the Lake of Fire. And the following passage is quite revealing in telling us what happens to the remainder of people, the unchosen:

> 4 And I saw thrones, and they sat upon them, and judgment was given unto them: and I saw the souls of them that were beheaded for the witness of Jesus, and for the word of God, and which had not worshipped the beast, neither his image, neither had received his mark upon their foreheads, or in their hands; and they lived and reigned with Christ a thousand years. 5 But the rest of the dead lived not again until the thousand years were finished. This is the first resurrection. 6 Blessed and holy is he that hath part in the first resurrection: on such the second death hath no power, but

they shall be priests of God and of Christ, and shall reign with him a thousand years. (Rev 20:4–6)

Verse five says the dead *live* (the first resurrection), and six says that the second death has no power over them who participate in the first resurrection. To repeat, *this is referring to the unchosen. It is referring to the remainder of people, the dead, raised at the end of the thousand years, which is the unchosen. So, the unchosen are raised and will experience no harm in the second death, which is the Lake of Fire.* Here Scripture is explicitly telling us that the Lake of Fire is not for killing. The dead cannot be eliminated by the Lake of Fire, or tortured in the Lake of Fire, and this, again, gives evidence that the Lake is for something other than GOD torturing and killing his creatures. The dead are those who do not have life, that is, the unsaved, those who are not salvific:

> 16 The heaven, even the heavens, are the LORD's: but the earth hath he given to the children of men. 17 *The dead praise not the LORD, neither any that go down into silence.* 18 But we will bless the LORD from this time forth and for evermore. (Ps 115:16–18)

And this next passage tells us that the dead are the *unsaved*, those who resurrect from the pre-Eschaton self-nonexistence as *condemned*.

> 5 For the living know that they shall die: but the dead know not any thing, neither have they any more a reward; for the memory of them is forgotten. (Eccl 9:5)

Only death and hell die in the Lake of Fire; humans are purified in it—in the baptizing Fire of GOD.

And consider one more of the seeming plethora of passages in Scripture that discuss how the dead *shall live* (future pointing):

> 17 Like as a woman with child, that draweth near the time of her delivery, is in pain, and crieth out in her pangs; so have we been in thy sight, O LORD. 18 We have been with child, we have been in pain, we have as it were brought forth wind; we have not wrought any deliverance in the earth; neither have the inhabitants of the world fallen. 19 Thy dead men shall live, together with my dead body shall they arise. Awake and sing, ye that dwell in dust: for thy dew is as the dew of herbs, and the earth shall cast out the dead. 20 Come, my people, enter thou into thy chambers, and shut thy doors about thee: hide thyself as it were for a little moment, until the indignation be overpast. (Isa 26:17–20)

Hyper-Calvinist Universal Salvation

This must be why the Lake of Fire of Revelation 21:8 is surrounded amid a context throughout Revelation 21 of the *afterlife* (21:4), in glory, and with no more tears. Revelation 21:8 is written as if the onset of the afterlife, well into the Eschaton, is when the unbelievers will be burned in the Consuming Lake of Fire. So, when it says in Revelation 2:11 that "He that overcometh shall not be hurt of the second death," it seems this can only mean that the saved overcome, and all the rest are cast into the Lake of Fire, *to be saved*, where the condemned *are* inevitably brought to amazement, during the second death (Isa 13:8) (this is part of the purification process, seemingly with the flesh being burned away; 1 Cor 5:5).

15

The Concept of Forever in Pre-Eschaton Underworldly Self-Nonexistence

As eluded to above, in the King James Version, all underworld references (Hades, Tartarus, Gehenna, Sheol, the grave) are often lumped into being referred to as "hell" and "the pit"[1] in both Testaments, but in the newer translations, the specific areas of the underworld are referred to by name. Lenchak writes, "only Gehenna truly designates a place of everlasting punishment for the wicked after death."[2] As discussed in a chapter above, before the underworlds are *all* destroyed by the Eschaton Fire (GOD), there is a period of self-nonexistence and self-annihilation (nonexistence of consciousness and self-experience) for apparently nearly all people, at the end of which GOD's Fire destroys all things (Eschaton Lake of Fire). So, the annihilation self-nonexistence is *temporary*, as has already been explained and established in this book—*but* there are a small number of references in the Bible to the pre-Eschaton self-nonexistence being "eternal," "everlasting," and "forever." This would appear to be in straightforward contradiction to the systematic theology of Hyper-Calvinist universal salvation presented to this point in this book. But upon closer analysis, we will find out that it is not a contradiction to Hyper-Calvinist universal salvation, and there is more to the picture. I will explore this issue next, and it will shed more light on the systematic theology of Hyper-Calvinist universal salvation.

These instances of "forever," "everlasting," and "eternal" are associated with the pre-Eschaton annihilation discussed above, and apparently is a

1. In the newer translations, "pit" is kept as "Sheol" (Balflour, "Into the Scriptural Import," 15).

2. Lenchack, "What's Biblical about . . . Hell?," 116.

Hyper-Calvinist Universal Salvation

specific type of annihilation. Of this type, the dormant and/or nonexistent soul of pre-Eschaton annihilation is in a gap in time that I call a "vertical infinity." What I want to discuss next is: there are periods of soul sleep and self-nonexistence annihilation in the pre-Eschaton underwordly regions, such as in Jonah 2, that are described as "everlasting," "forever," or "eternal," when they are not really, not actually, everlasting, forever, eternal, in the horizontal sense of the timeline. More simply, there is a gap of nonexistence of the self, which in some cases are described as an *infinite amount of time* (everlasting, forever, eternal) in Scripture, when it *is not* an unending (everlasting, forever, eternal) span on the timeline. So, what is going on here?

The answer to this question is given in Jonah 2. The hole in time, or what I will call the "vertical infinity," involves a sort of infinity of experience—in the void of timelessness, in the nonexistence of being in a crack in time—in a nonreality of self, in the underworldly loss of awareness. To explore this, we need to look at the definition and nature of the word "forever" in a specific passage, Jonah 2, since in that passage a definition of the concept of "forever" is set for all of Scripture, *specifically* as the concept of "forever" is found in the context of hell and the underworld realities or condemnation states in Scripture. And the definition set by Jonah 2:6 indicates *which type* of "forever" is denoted when Scripture refers to condemnation, death, and the underworlds. Some readers may be surprised to see the indication in the previous sentence, that there are *different types* of forever, but it is straightforward to understand how this is the case, as I will do next.

The word "forever" appears at verse 6 of Jonah 2:

> 6 I went down to the bottoms of the mountains; the earth with her bars was about me for *ever*: yet hast thou brought up my life from corruption, O LORD my God. 7 When my soul fainted within me I remembered the LORD: and my prayer came in unto thee, into thine holy temple. (Jon 2:6–7)

Virtually all Bible versions, from old to new, use the word "forever" in verse 6. What is denoted by the word "forever" is Jonah's duration in the belly of the sea beast (verse 2: "belly of hell"), even though Jonah's time ("forever") of being in the underworld, where he is in a fainting-annihilation state, is *only three days*. The self-nonexistence and annihilation of the consciousness and/or soul is discussed as being "forever" ("everlasting," "eternal," etc.), but *it is not*, since on the timeline, it is only a three-day gap between two lives: a corrupted life, and a life coming into salvation. Loosely put, and poetically put (due to there being a lack of better words), what it appears is being expressed in Scripture is that within this gap of annihilation of self comes breakage from past, a bringing of newness to the person at the first resurrection, due to a clean break from physical attachment, and a consequent capacity to be with GOD or to look at GOD, at varying levels of intensity.

Interestingly, Jonah's time in the underworld, the deep, the realm of the dead, did *not* lead into the Eschaton: he awoke *before* the Eschaton. This reveals that people can go in and out of annihilation phases *before* death of the physical body (that is, *before* the last and final annihilation phase that *does* lead into the Eschaton), but where the self-haecceity and qualia, which defines what a person is, is intact before and after the annihilations: whenever self/consciousness of a person, a soul, exists (outside of any pre-Eschaton annihilation(s)), it can be described as having its same self-haecceity and qualia, and the LORD can bring those in and out of existence as He wills and chooses. So, there are some phases of self-nonexistence that can happen before the death of the body. In other words, there are some phases of annihilation that happen before a person's body dies, and before the long annihilation self-nonexistence that leads into, and is not reversed until, the resurrection of those who are salvific before the thousand years, and the resurrection of sinners at the first resurrection after the thousand years. What, precisely, any such initial self-nonexistence phases might be like is not speculated in this book, other than one comment, as follows. These earlier annihilations have some differences from the final annihilation at body death, because that final self-nonexistence leads to the resurrection at the Eschaton (Rev 20:4–6), and any theorized earlier annihilations do not, and thus would be a different annihilating than the final annihilation.[3] But

---

3. It appears there are levels of intensity (perhaps in terms of frequency or length), and perhaps stages, of increasing annihilation and self-nonexistence revealed in Scripture. For example, a chosen person who is salvific in this pre-Eschaton physical reality would have undergone an annihilation, a being born-again of self, into being reborn in Christ (Gal 2:20), where the old is gone and the *new* has come (2 Cor 5:17). For the old to be gone, it would have to cease to exist, and a new self comes into existence. There is a clean rift between these two selves, to where the new self has to be brought into existence (out of nothing, but born of GOD). The same haecceity and qualia of self would be recreated, after a gap of nonexistence. Being born again (such as with the conversion experience), in the physical dimension, does not have the finality and intensity of the first resurrection of the Eschaton, but nevertheless, something like the conversion experience could comprise an earlier, less intense fractal of the post-body annihilation and the first resurrection at the Eschaton. And it seems that Jacob wrestling with GOD also is an example of pre-Eschaton pre-body-death annihilation. With Jacob, we have an instance where a person sees GOD and cannot live, since no man can see GOD and live (Ex 33:20,

Hyper-Calvinist Universal Salvation

our concern here is not the theology of annihilation and self-nonexistence; rather, our concern is this: why Jonah is described as being in the underworld "forever," when he was only there for *three days*.

Before the Eschaton transformation, the states of a person are all finite on the horizontal timeline, where the person moves along from creation of the soul before time (Eph 1:4), aimed toward the Eschaton. But there is a change of this horizontal direction in time when the person ceases to exist (self-nonexistence): there is a gap in reality (a gap in *experienced* reality and time), a breach in existence (in the *experience* of existence)—there is a hole in time.[4] What I am proposing is that the Bible contains a horizontal timeline of the soul and self, infinitely into the future, from the point of the creation of the soul before time, up to and through the Eschaton, on into the infinity of afterlife (which involves an unendingness, like a mathematical number line into positive infinity)—*but* where at some point leading into the Eschaton, there is a cut, a gap, forming a chasm, a pit (the often used Old Testament term), a void, a break, in the timeline, which I am calling the "vertical infinity," where this pre-Eschaton slice in the timeline is a vertical movement in time, which is *downward*, down *into* the timeline, rather than across it. This delving deeply into the timeline, rather than continuing to flow across it, functions like a pause, a stoppage, of the flow of

---

also see 1 Tim 6:16). But Jacob did have life preserved (saltiness): he was annihilated somewhere during the wrestling with GOD event, and then *preserved* (recall Mk 9:49).

> 30 And Jacob called the name of the place Peniel: for I have seen God face to face, and my life is *preserved*. (Genesis 32:30)

"Preserved" is an interesting word to use here. We will see in the next chapter that Mark 9:49, where the salt, the preserver, is what is involved with the Eschaton Fire (Lake of Fire), the Fire that *everyone* is affected by. I drawn connection here of Genesis 32:30 and Mark 9:49, in that there is only one preserving Fire—all other fire does not preserve—so the verses must be referring, ultimately, to the same Fire: the only Fire that preserves. So, this passage about Jacob wrestling with GOD seems to be a fractal of the Eschaton, a micro-Eschaton during the pre-Eschaton time, like Jonah. Interesting that he received a new name, Israel, right after; his new self needed a new name, since the old one seemingly did not apply to the new one. There are disruptions in physical reality like these, moments of singularity annihilation, like the Mount Sinai events, Moses with Pharoah, to give a third example, that involve death, annihilation, and rebirth, all within pre-Eschaton time, and all within the time of the physical dimension.

4. The way I have written this sentence, the reader may have noticed, implies that time is a figment of experience only, and not necessarily a mind-independent entity outside of experience. If the reader does not prefer this sort of metaphysics of time, one need merely sidestep what I have done here, and presume that time is mind-independent, as that will not affect the outcomes of anything concluded in this book.

The Concept of Forever in Pre-Eschaton Underworldly Self-Nonexistence

time, where we are considering the timeline, the flow of time, to be roughly analogous to the Real number line (that is, the set of all rational and irrational numbers on the number line), for example, where one probes *into* the infinities of moments between any two moments, rather than moving across the timeline through the moments. It is as if the self and/or soul has stopped flowing through the number line, from 1, to 2, to 3, to 4 . . . to instead delving deeply into all the infinity of moments between two times, such as between 1 and 2: 1.5, 1.25, 1.125, and so on, infinitely. It is as if the soul has started endlessly dividing *into* the timeline, rather than flowing *across* it and *through* it. This *dividing into* would function as a time stoppage, or like a gap, a cut, or bottomless *pit* (to put it in KJV wording), *in* the flow of time (a gap in horizontal time). So, in Jonah 2, we see that a three-day span is referred to as being "forever," which may seem like a contradiction, but what appears to be happening is that Jonah's movement through time shifted from horizontal to vertical, delving into a gap of self-nonexistence and/or soul sleep.

But there is more light to shed on this matter, and to reveal the perfect logic of Scripture. You may not have noticed that people use different senses of the word "forever" in their daily lives, and one of the ways they commonly use it is referring to a timespan that is not infinite, but one that is *finite*. Let me give an example. Consider this sentence: "I have been waiting *forever* for my burger and fries in this drive-thru." The person saying this is referring to a finite timespan with the word "forever," and this appears to be what Jonah is doing in Jonah 2:6. We can see both finite and infinite timespan references in *Merriam-Webster*'s definition of "forever," where the noun definition of "forever" appears to be how the word is used in Jonah 2:6. Here are the definitions of "forever" from *Merriam-Webster*:

> Forever (adverb)
> 1: for a limitless time
> 2: at all times: continually
> Forever (noun)
> : a seemingly interminable time: excessively long[5]

Notice how the noun definition specifically *does not* involve a concept of *unendingness*. On the timeline (the horizontal time stream), the noun definition of "forever" does not involve a horizontal unendingness—which I refer to as a "mathematical infinity," or "mathematical infinity of time," in

---

5. *Merriam-Webster.com Dictionary*, s.v. "forever," https://www.merriam-webster.com/dictionary/forever.

Hyper-Calvinist Universal Salvation

this book. The adverb definitions *do* contain the concept of being horizontally unending: mathematically extending into future infinity on the timeline, from the start of the soul's existence, to the Eschaton, and into the mathematical infinity of time of the afterlife. But the noun definition plainly does not involve the concept of being without end. The noun definition is more like a pause, and therefore like a gap in time, a hole in the flow of time, which can be unpaused, and which one can be pulled out of. The gap is created by an episode or epoch of self-nonexistence, which functions as some sort of an eternity and/or everlastingness during the pausing of time experience, into nonexistence of the self and/or soul. As we have seen in this book in several verses and passages of Scripture, especially in the older translations (AKJV), hell is referred to as a "pit," which is a synonym for "hole." This hole in time is a pit, a cavity, or gap, inside of which is an aspect of, a part of, the infinity of hell referred to in Scripture:

> Yet thou shalt be brought down to hell, to the sides of the pit. (Isa 14:15)

The adverb and noun definitions therefore appear to *contradict* each other, wherein only one of these sorts of definitions from *Merriam-Webster* (adverb or noun) can be applied to Jonah 2:6. It appears self-evident that the noun definition applies to Jonah 2:6, and if it does, that would seem to set the definition for the concept of "forever," in the context of condemnation and underworldly existence of souls, *throughout Scripture*, as being described by the noun definition of "forever": a vertical infinity, or a gap, in the timeline, which is eventually reversed. This noun usage of the word "forever" would be consistent with other places in this book where we find that GOD refers to times differently than we ordinary humans do, and specifically he refers to them as being the opposite of what we would: a day is a thousand years and in Jonah 2, three days is a forever (vertical infinity).

The noun definition of the concept of forever hell in Scripture would appear to bind all uses of the concept of forever hell, underworldly existence, and damnation in Scripture to being the noun definition: uncomfortably long, but not a mathematical infinity of temporally horizontal unendingness. And this noun usage of "forever" would apply to any and all instances of "hell," "damnation," "the pit," and so on in Scripture. Why this is so is because if all instances of foreverness in Scripture surrounding hell and condemnation *did not* conform to the noun definition, then *some* instances of hell damnation in Scripture would involve a mathematical

The Concept of Forever in Pre-Eschaton Underworldly Self-Nonexistence

infinity of a temporal forever, and others would not, which would lead to hell damnation (pre-Eschaton self-nonexistence) as being simultaneously both horizontally infinite and *not* horizontally infinite, which would be a contradiction.

For those reasons, all instances of foreverness in the context of underworld existence in Scripture will be considered to be noun definitions: at least in some cases of pre-Eschaton self-nonexistence in Scripture, an aspect of hell, does *not* involve a horizontal infinity of time, but rather an infinity of time and/or experience that is more like a hole or *pit* in the stream of time. The concept of foreverness in Scripture here discussed as noun-like (a foreverness that can be interrupted, stopped), *only* is found in Scripture in the context of hell, the underworld (Sheol, Hades, Gehenna, hell, the grave, land of the dead), condemnation, damnation, and possibly paradise (where for whatever precisely paradise is, it is apparently not identical to heaven, and is under the earth), but not in the context of the upcoming heavenly existence in the afterlife. And contrastingly, Scripture uses the *adverbial* definition of "forever" (eternal, everlasting, unending, etc.) in the context of, and when discussing, the upcoming forever, post-Eschaton afterlife for souls (all souls) with GOD, and also *within, inside of* (Eccl 12:7), GOD. Specifically, that is because there are no Scripture passages that involve a soul, a person, being *removed from* the state of heavenly afterlife, in the direct presence of GOD, seeing him face to face, after our old bodies are destroyed and we are given new bodies. Therefore, the concept of foreverness is used in opposite ways in Scripture when discussing hell and annihilation self-nonexistence (pre-Eschaton), on the one hand, and heavenly afterlife in the kingdom of light (Rev 22:3–5), in Christ (post-Eschaton), on the other. We are never told that the afterlife in glory has an end, but in Scripture we are told that the foreverness of pre-Eschaton self-nonexistence (hell, Sheol, damnation, condemnation, the grave, land of the dead, etc.) *does* have an end (Jon 2:6–7; Rev. 20:14).

So, what is going on is that GOD removes souls from non-heavenly states to bring them into an infinite afterlife with him. Again, there has to be a cessation of existence of *any and every* soul, in the soul's time stream of existence (I am referring again to the pre-Eschaton period of self-nonexistence), when it goes from the old self to the new, from corrupt to incorrupt. According to Scripture, this contributes to the cessation of the old self, and the bringing in of the new. This distinction, of foreverness (adverb) in glory/afterlife versus foreverness (noun) in hell damnation

Hyper-Calvinist Universal Salvation

(self-nonexistence), shows the contrast of the two types of infinities of foreverness, described as opposites in Scripture. From what has been found to this point, even if there *are* any condemnation states described as *forever, unending*, in the Bible, any such state would nevertheless have to reduce to the vertical infinity of underworld experience, and could only function as a gap in time, and/or a self-nonexistence, *that is reversed* when one is lifted out of the underworld (discussed in a chapter below), and not anything like the popular view of hell.

Before unchosen humans are saved, they are destroyed (annihilated, nonexistent). Above we discussed this with Matthew 10:28, but the same concept appears to be found in the following passages:

> 1 Come, and let us return unto the LORD: for he hath torn, and he will heal us; he hath smitten, and he will bind us up. 2 After two days will he revive us: in the third day he will raise us up, and we shall live in his sight. 3 Then shall we know, if we follow on to know the LORD: his going forth is prepared as the morning; and he shall come unto us as the rain, as the latter and former rain unto the earth. (Hos 6:1–3)

> Thou turnest man to destruction; and sayest, Return, ye children of men. (Ps 90:3)

The underworld annihilation is, at its deepest core, an issue of the deep inner mind, our immaterial spirit,[6] the soul: "The waters compassed me about,

---

6. I imagine many readers of this book are, philosophically speaking, physicalists (reject the existence of nonphysical entities), whether they know it or not, and therefore feel squeamish when I refer to the self as an "immaterial spirit." But the fact is, if one looks inward to look at their consciousness, it has virtually no material/physical qualities, and appears precisely to be a nonphysical spirit (nonphysical meaning that it merely does not have material qualities: extension, temporality, emergence and fading away, surface and solidity, they are empirical, and so forth). The extremely famous philosopher John Searle discusses how consciousness *seems to be* mysterious and spiritual, as if that is an illusion, and what we are "seeing" when we look at consciousness introspectively cannot be trusted, and that does not represent what consciousness is like (Searle, *Mystery of Consciousness*, xii.). When we introspect and look at our own consciousnesses, we find that they look precisely and thoroughly like immaterial spirits, *not* at all like material things, such as water or bricks. If one tries to describe a feeling, for example, phenomenologically, one cannot even form words or sentences about it, to describe what it is, what it is made of, its substance, if it even has such, since a feeling does not have any physical qualities to describe, but only qualities that are not physical (nonphysical qualities). This is the opposite of the standard, and in ways, the only acceptable, line of thought that professional academics will consider in discussing consciousness, which seems to me, surprising. So, in other words, they deny what they observe directly. This would be

The Concept of Forever in Pre-Eschaton Underworldly Self-Nonexistence

even to the soul: the depth closed me round about" (Jon 2:5). In Amos 9:3, the deep, the covering, is a place that covers a person from being *seen* by GOD. We see the same happening in Jonah 2:4: "I am cast out of thy sight." This would seem to be a very important concept, and likely has something to do with the nonexistence, the annihilation, of self, when in the vertical infinity. At the soul level, being in the underworld *first* causes Jonah to erroneously believe GOD is not with him (one can never be without GOD, even if in the underworlds or in hell; see Ps 139:7–8; Rom 8:38–39; Eph 1:23), not reaching into his soul. And since when GOD looks at us, he looks at the *innermost* self, our soul (1 Sam 16:7), then in underworld scenarios, GOD is apparently *not* looking at the person's inner self and soul. Perhaps Jonah could feel how GOD was not looking at him, causing him to feel as if GOD was not with him.

We see that in the deep of underworldly existence, there Jonah finally *remembers* GOD (Jon 2:7). Without consciousness, presumably Jonah could not pray (he prayed *before* the loss of consciousness, before the fainting; see Jon 2:1–2). So, the prayer that came to the LORD in Jonah 2:7 must have been prayed *before* Jonah went unconscious and presumably nonexistent, which is the prayer we are told about in Jonah 2:2: "I cried by reason of my affliction unto the LORD, and he heard me." So, it was the *hardship* that Jonah was in that caused him to pray, wherein the LORD simultaneously heard the prayer. Here is another passage, about David, who was in sorrow, also asking the LORD to hear him, so as to avoid death sleep:

> 1 How long wilt thou forget me, O LORD? for ever? how long wilt thou hide thy face from me? 2 How long shall I take counsel in my soul, having sorrow in my heart daily? how long shall mine enemy be exalted over me? 3 Consider and hear me, O LORD my God: lighten mine eyes, lest I sleep the sleep of death; 4 lest mine enemy say, I have prevailed against him; and those that trouble me rejoice when I am moved. 5 But I have trusted in thy mercy; my heart shall rejoice in thy salvation. 6 I will sing unto the LORD, because he hath dealt bountifully with me. (Ps 13)

But in Jonah 2:7, *which is a later time*, after the prayer, presumably while Jonah was asleep (fainted, representing self-nonexistence and loss of

---

analogous to a scientist denying what they most directly see, such as that the sky is blue, or that objects fall downward to earth when dropped. In other words, professional academics, in the present age, analyze consciousness anti-scientifically (or perhaps in better words, *anti-experientially*: not according to how it is plainly experienced) (see Grupp, *GOD-Faith*, chapter 1, for copious discussion on this topic).

consciousness), we are told that it was *then* that the prayer went *inside* of GOD, it *"came in* unto thee." So there appears to be, at least in the case of Jonah, some sort of delay across different times and events, seemingly representing the gap of the soul, the nonexistence of the soul. Here is the sequence of events:

1. Jonah prays *and is heard by* the LORD.
2. Later, Jonah has fainted, representing self-nonexistence (absence of self and self-awareness), where, at the very least, some significant core aspect of his soul ceases to exist (it has died, while in the belly of hell, the realm of death).
3. During Jonah's fainting annihilation, where Jonah underwent a death, his old self gone, the prayer goes *into* GOD, *inside of* the being of GOD.

From this analysis, the belly of hell, from which a person is resurrected from by the LORD, involves ceasing to exist, a true death, where, in the LORD, in *looking at* the soul, not just hearing it, the person is resurrected. The person is brought back from the annihilation mentioned in Matthew 10:28. From the fainting and loss of functioning of Jonah's soul we come to the conclusion that he momentarily ceases to exist, denoted by the noun definition of "forever." This cessation of the existence of the soul appears to be a core element to a person being in the core (belly) of hell. This is what is involved in the infinity of hell, at least for many, a vertical infinity of self-nonexistence, before the Eschaton and before salvation.

16

Passages That May Appear to Contradict Hyper-Calvinist Universal Salvation

BEFORE WE CONTINUE IN exploring the systematic theology of Hyper-Calvinist universal salvation, I want to explore a few passages that could, at a first glance, appear to be contrary to Hyper-Calvinist universal salvation, but where, on a closer look, they do not.

Consider this first passage:

> 8 Wherefore if thy hand or thy foot offend thee, cut them off, and cast them from thee: it is better for thee to enter into life halt or maimed, rather than having two hands or two feet to be cast into everlasting fire. 9 And if thine eye offend thee, pluck it out, and cast it from thee: it is better for thee to enter into life with one eye, rather than having two eyes to be cast into hell fire. (Matt 18:8–9)

The two verses are roughly duplicates in their message, but the passage uses "everlasting fire" (αἰώνιον πῦρ) at the end of the first verse, and "hell fire" (γέενναν πυρός) at the end of the second. Used in this way, it could make it appear as if the two are interchangeable, and thus as if "everlasting fire" (unending) = "hell fire" (not unending). If that were correct, it would involve contradiction. But we can see from the Greek that these are different concepts, one being Gehenna/hell fire, that is finite in time, and the other unending fire. We found in earlier chapters that the "everlasting fire" of verse 8 cannot be hell (Gehenna), since hell is not everlasting, and since hell will soon be destroyed in the Lake of Fire, along with all of the heavens and the earth (2 Pet 3:10; Mark 13:31). The only *everlasting fire* is GOD, the Lake of Fire (Rev 20:10), so if "everlasting fire" were equal to "hell fire"

Hyper-Calvinist Universal Salvation

in this passage, the text would reduce to absurdism. The obvious solution, then, is to, as we have in previous chapters, understand that "everlasting fire" ≠ "hell fire." Then the obvious question is would be: why is Matthew 18:8–9 denoting "everlasting fire" and "hell fire" in a way that it makes them look interchangeable and identical? The message in Matthew 18:8–9 is of this form: it is better to have not-X now than to later have X at location Y (where Y = GOD). And what changes from verse 8 to 9 is the Y variable, where it looks like this:

> It is better to have not-X_1 now than to later have X_1 at location GOD.[1] (verse 8).
>
> It is better to have not-X_2 now than to later have X_2 at location not-GOD.[2] (verse 9).

Apparently, GOD is saying in this passage, from verses 8 to 9, that regardless of where one goes, it is better to have weakness (not-X) than strength (X), regardless of whether one is in the condemned state and/or pre-Eschaton (location not-GOD), or in the salvific state (location GOD). It is as if GOD is saying in this passage: "Regardless of whether you are in a state where I have not started to mold you, or you have salvation, it is best to act in weakness than in strength" (see 2 Cor 12:9).

In the King James Bible, the word "hell," when in the context of the underworld, often is used to describe the entire underworld and all its areas, whether the fiery torture locations (also called hell, or Gehenna) or the non-fiery locations (such as Hades, realm of sleep and/or self-nonexistence). So, King James readers who do not know the Greek will often not know which section of the underworld is being referred to. Note, however, that this is not the case in verse 9 of Matthew 18, which denotes a *fiery* area of the underworld (Gehenna). And it is the case in the following passage that, at first glance, it may appear to be in contradiction with the systematic Hyper-Calvinist universal salvation theology of this book, since the verse claims there are people in hell:

> And the sea gave up the dead which were in it; and death and *hell* delivered up the dead *which were in them*: and they were judged every man according to their works. (Rev 20:13)

---

1. Here, I am saying that the location Y is equal to GOD: Y=GOD. So, if one is at location GOD, one is inside of GOD. But specifically, by "location GOD" I am referring to feeling the presence of GOD. Same with the next statement.

2. By "not GOD" I mean not aware of GOD's presence.

Passages That May Appear to Contradict Hyper-Calvinist Universal Salvation

The word for "hell" here is ᾅδης (Hadēs), which is not the fiery region of the underworld,[3] but is rather the location of pre-Eschaton sleep and self-nonexistence, wherein which Revelation 20:13 would not involve any people in a fiery underworld or endless torture. As stated in chapter 1, no scripture supports the popular view of hell, and at no time are there people being consciously tortured by GOD by fire, and thus Revelation 20:13 does not contradict the systematic theology of Hyper-Calvinist universal salvation. What is more curious is why the King James Version is, it might seem, more vague about its description of the underworld, unless, on the other hand, the King James Version is revealing something about the underworld and about hell that the post-Textus Bible translations do not. It is as if the King James reading smears the concepts of the underworld regions together, but the post-Textus Bibles do not. Hell is a larger concept in both the King James Version, as well as the post-Textus Bibles, than just being an underworld, and scripturally, it is not labeled as one specific location under the world only, as in the popular view of hell. In the King James Version, hell is more widespread, including into the upper areas on the earth's surface. So, perhaps the KJV smearing the concept of hell, from just being in the underworld in one confine, to being all through the underworld and upper surface, is a reference to the world being reserved for fire at the Eschaton, and thus already kindled now, pre-Eschaton (Deut 4:36; 32:22; 2 Pet 3:7; Luke 12:49).

And lastly, consider the following passage, which was discussed above.

> 2 And many of them that sleep in the dust of the earth shall awake, some to everlasting life, and some to shame and everlasting contempt. 3 And they that be wise shall shine as the brightness of the firmament; and they that turn many to righteousness as the stars for ever and ever. (Dan 12:2–3)

I believe this passage is a reference to how a person *awakens from* the underworld sleep (annihilation, self-nonexistence), since verse 2 says "shall awake." At the point of awakening, the person will not yet be on the other side of being condemned: not yet put into the Fire for refining and salvation. Above we learned that in the Parable of the Tares, people are resurrected (the first resurrection), judged, and if put in the line of the goats, then put in place for being burned in the Lake of Fire. So, I believe that the only scenario that fits the description of what is going on here is that a

---

3. In chapter 5 above I discussed why Luke 16:23, the reference to Hades in the Parable of Lazarus and the Beggar, is not a reference to an *actual* fiery underworld area.

person has been brought back into consciousness (self-existence), so they are no longer annihilated, but they are still pre-salvific. This seems to be why this state is one of being in "everlasting contempt," or vertical contempt, rather than everlasting (vertical) destruction. To state that a person is in "everlasting contempt" is like saying they have awakened into forever being in a state of dejection in the face of GOD. It does not seem that the word "everlasting," in "everlasting contempt," is referring to some sort of state of afterglow of vertical infinity and self-nonexistence (for lack of better words) that the soul has just awakened from. The vertical infinity is about self-nonexistence, and upon being awakened, the self *has* existence: mental content again floods the soul, thus leading to the stream of consciousness, which the soul has awakened into. So, the word "everlasting" in "everlasting contempt" must be connected to, and pointed at, the state of the self's existence (everlasting existence) upon awakening in the Eschaton, where it will be positioned for the Lake of Fire, wherein it will live forever. In that plain reading of the verse, the word "everlasting" seems to fit well, and the word "contempt" must refer to the endless state of awareness that the self is worthless, which seemingly would be known to the self through every moment of the mathematical infinity of afterlife in glory.

Next, consider Mark 9:43–50, which is also another passage that could appear to contradict Hyper-Calvinist universal salvation, but which instead gives greater clarification to it. I believe this one could be a primary one that leads to some of the erroneous ideas of the popular view of hell. Here is the passage:

> 43 And if thy hand offend thee, cut it off: it is better for thee to enter into life maimed, than having two hands to go into *hell*, into the fire that never shall be quenched: 44 where their worm dieth not, and the fire is *not quenched*. 45 And if thy foot offend thee, cut it off: it is better for thee to enter halt into life, than having two feet to be cast into *hell*, into *the fire that never shall be quenched*: 46 where their worm dieth not, and the *fire is not quenched*. 47 And if thine eye offend thee, pluck it out: it is better for thee to enter into the kingdom of God with one eye, than having two eyes to be cast into *hell fire*: 48 where their worm dieth not, and the fire is not quenched. 49 For *every one shall be salted with fire*, and every sacrifice shall be salted with salt. 50 Salt is good: but if the salt have lost his saltness, wherewith will ye season it? Have salt in yourselves, and have peace one with another. (Mark 9:43–50)

Passages That May Appear to Contradict Hyper-Calvinist Universal Salvation

I have heard some scholars suggesting that the salting referred to in verse 49 refers to using salt on the ground to prevent the growing of plants (Deut 29:23). There are differing references to the use of salt in Scripture (see 2 Kgs 2:21), but regardless, Mark 9:49 is referring to *salt bringing fire*, as if salting leads to fire, and that does not seem comparable to putting salt on the ground to prevent plant growth. Mark 9:49 is talking about people, not plants. But the key is that verse 49 says *everyone* is salted, so that indicates that the salting has to do with GOD, since only GOD can have an effect, of any sort, on *every* person, and therefore this does not have to do with actual usage of the resource of physical salt by people in the Middle East in the ancient world, where regardless, salting cannot bring about fire in the first place. A better context for the discussion of salt, also from the words of Jesus, is Matthew 5:13–16:

> 13 Ye are the salt of the earth: but if the salt have lost his savour, wherewith shall it be salted? it is thenceforth good for nothing, but to be cast out, and to be trodden under foot of men. 14 Ye are the light of the world. A city that is set on an hill cannot be hid. 15 Neither do men light a candle, and put it under a bushel, but on a candlestick; and it giveth light unto all that are in the house. 16 Let your light so shine before men, that they may see your good works, and glorify your Father which is in heaven. (Matt 5:13–16)

It seems pretty straightforward here that salt is in the context of salvation, and of having the fire of zeal for GOD, so, it seems self-evident that salt is not related to literal usage in either Mark 9:49 or Matthew 5:13. It appears since salt does not lead to fire, and that people are not identical to physical salt, so Scripture makes it clear that this is metaphorical, and not to be literal,[4] since

human persons ≠ physical grains of salt,

So, I will move on from this faulty concept.

---

4. In holing a literalist account of all of Scripture, I hold that passages that are metaphorical are *overtly so*, so that there cannot be confusion, such as in saying that people are salted with fire. There is no way that concept can make any sense if, for example, table salt is being referred to, and therefore, it can only be viewed as a teaching tool, not a literal happening. And Jesus refers to saltiness as involving a zestiness like when salting food (see Matt 5:13), thus establishing the metaphorical usage of salt. We saw this previously in discussing the Parable of Lazarus a the Beggar. Similarly, GOD does not *literally* expect people to cut off their hands if they cause them to sin (Matt 5:30), since *he* did not do anything like that, nor any of his prophets in Scripture, and since Jesus did not advocate or demonstrate any sort of self-harm anywhere resembling that.

Hyper-Calvinist Universal Salvation

A first question, regarding Mark 9:43–50, is which fire is being discussed here: underworld fire (hell), or the Consuming Fire (GOD) of the Eschaton? The answer is that *both* are being discussed. Mark 9:43–50 blurs the lines between these two fires. The references to "hell" in this passage are the Greek γέενναν, or Gehenna, in both the ancient Bibles (such as KJV) and the modern translations. Gehenna in the Bible is theorized by scholars as referring to a valley near Jerusalem, and a place of burning corpses, which does not match up well with the description of the popular view of hell (Gehenna is not *inside* the earth, for example). The Greek word for "fire" throughout the passage is πῦρ, which does not necessarily mean *only* Gehenna and/or a hell-like fire, but has associations with being the *eternal* fire (which would indicate the Lake of Fire, since hell is not eternal, but is *ended* in the Lake of Fire, absorbed into the Lake of Fire), also related to the heat from the sun, having to do with *lightning* (note Luke 17:24; Matt 24:27; 28:3; Rev 8:5; 11:19; 16:18) or fire from GOD. In Mark 9:48, the fire of hell is described as *"not* (οὐ) quenched" (σβέννυμι, suppressed, put out), which is the second time the hellfire is mentioned as being unquenchable in the passage. But then, interestingly, at verse 49, we see a significant change of subject. Verses 43–48 are about hellfire, so it might seem that verse 49 is also about hellfire, but it can't be, for multiple reasons. Verse 49 moves from present tense ("is not quenched," "never shall be quenched") to future-pointing: *everyone shall be salted with fire*. But we know that not everyone goes into hell (John 5:24), and there is no account of a person being in a fiery hell in the Bible. So, verse 49 has shifted into discussing the Consuming Fire (Lake of Fire, GOD, YHWH, Θεός), since GOD is the Fire that preserves everyone, and Mark 9:49 is referring to a fire that preserves *everyone*. And there is further evidence for this in how verses 49 and 50 refer to the Fire being a salting, where this would shift the focus from being about destruction, to implications GOD's covenant with humans, and about preserving (such as salt being a preservative in the ancient world), or seasoning (adding zest, savoriness). But the Greek word for fire in 9:49 remains the same as used in verses 43–48. The same wording for fire in Greek is used to describe both hellfire and GOD-Fire (Lake of Fire): different fires (eternal and noneternal) are both described by πῦρ. The fire of hell and the Fire of GOD have very differing qualities (torture versus baptism, noneternal versus eternal, and so forth), wherein the two are opposites, but there is apparently enough resemblance between the two (such as that both are *fiery* in their morphology) that each are labeled as like the fire that we humans experience in our physical dimension; both are similar enough that πῦρ can be used to describe both.

Mark 9:43–48 has three references to hellfire, each one referring to hell as being *unquenchable*, implying that the hellfire is everlasting. If what has been written in the previous chapters is correct, that would inform us that the unquenchable hellfire would be a vertical infinity, since it's in the context of *forever* condemnation (vertically forever, Zenoically forever). If hell were a horizontal infinity in Mark 9:43–48, it would contradict the concept of forever in hell (KJV), the pit, realm of the dead, in Jonah 2:6, which states that the forever of condemnation is a *vertical* infinity of time, not a *horizontal* infinity of time. Even if Mark 9:43–48 used words like "eternal," "everlasting," or "forever" to describe the hellfire in this passage, it could still only refer to the vertical forever of Jonah 2, lest a singularity of logical breakdown emerge out of the cogent matrix of the systematic theology of Scripture. Since it is in the context of condemnation (hell), we would know the fire of verses 43–48 are not referring to the Fire if GOD, the eternal Consuming Fire, which verse 49 must be referring to, if Scripture is to avoid a singularity of contradiction.

17

GOD Pulls Souls Out of the Vertical Infinity (Self-Nonexistence, Annihilation)

THE PICTURE WE HAVE before us is one where at the interface between (1) pre-Eschaton reality in this physical dimension, and (2) the Eschaton, there exists an infinity of depth into self-nonexistence, out of which the condemned soul is resurrected at the Eschaton, to thereafter see GOD directly, and to be immolated in the Lake of GOD's Fire. Why would a person fall into the vertical infinity, and further, how is the person removed from it(as in Rev 20:13)? If GOD is omnipotent and omnisovereign, then the only answer can be that GOD puts the person into vertical infinity, and then pulls them out. Since he is in control of all things (according to the Hyper-Calvinist—and therefore occasionalist/omnicausal—theological model of reality that this book unveils), and since apart from him we can do nothing (John 15:5), then the only answer as to why a person can be brought into, and out of, vertical infinity (self-nonexistence), is by the sovereign GOD's ordaining and predestinating it all to happen.

Before the self-annihilation, the person was moving along the horizonal timeline, experiencing and feeling a time flow, moving from one *discreet* moment to the next, analogous to a person moving from one integer to the next on the number line.[1] The underworld existence between pre-Eschaton

---

1. Some may notice that this is roughly the scenario of what is called Planck time in quantum physics. This would lead to a scenario where the present moment is flashing in and out of existence, as time flows. That all particles of reality are flashing in and out of existence is a standard position amongst quantum physicists (see Kane, *Supersymmetry*, 19; Davies, *Superforce*, 104–5), and it leads to a position where between *any two moments is an annihilation*, which can only be reversed by GOD, who would therein bring every moment into existence out of nothing at every moment: "Behold, I make all things new" (Rev 21:5).

GOD Pulls Souls Out of the Vertical Infinity

physical existence and the Eschaton involves a loss of consciousness, where in the depths, the soul hears the LORD again, the LORD hears them, and at the deepest point, the point of self-nonexistence, GOD brings back the soul, ultimately to bring it into the Eschaton for salvation. He pulls it out of the underworld. We just analyzed Jonah 2 on these matters, and now consider another such Scripture:

> 7 Whither shall I go from thy spirit? or whither shall I flee from thy presence? 8 If I ascend up into heaven, thou art there: if I make my bed in hell, behold, thou art there. 9 If I take the wings of the morning, and dwell in the uttermost parts of the sea; 10 even there shall thy hand lead me, and thy right hand shall hold me. 11 If I say, Surely the darkness shall cover me; even the night shall be light about me. 13 Yea, the darkness hideth not from thee; but the night shineth as the day: the darkness and the light are both alike to thee. For thou hast possessed my reins: thou hast covered me in my mother's womb. 14 I will praise thee; for I am fearfully and wonderfully made: marvellous are thy works; and that my soul knoweth right well. 15 My substance was not hid from thee, when I was made in secret, and curiously wrought in the lowest parts of the earth. 16 Thine eyes did see my substance, yet being unperfect; and in thy book all my members were written, which in continuance were fashioned, when as yet there as none of them. 17 How precious also are thy thoughts unto me, O God! how great is the sum of them! (Ps 139:7–17)

We see in verses 7, 11, and 12 that we cannot be apart from GOD (see also Rom 8:38–39), even if in hell (verse 8), and then in this context we see a reference in verse 9 to this hell experience being the "uttermost parts of the sea," a reference to going to the depths. Then verse 15 appears to indicate that in that innermost depth we are *formed*: in the deepest ocean, in the underworld, like Jonah, we are worked, transformed, amid our (pre-Eschaton) time of imperfection, corruption (verse 16). We see multiple references to, at the deepest points of night, the day being sensed, witnessed: in the deepest night, the light is found—the Light shineth in the darkness (John 1:5). This is the overall theme of hell and damnation discussed in this book as residing in Scripture: at the deepest verticality of hell/damnation annihilation (forever), GOD is revealed as the soul is moved out of that vertical infinity (see Ps 139:8; Rev 20:14; Ps 2:27; and Ps 16:10).

Mathematically speaking, there are always infinite numbers between any two numbers, between any two points, on the Real number line. This

Hyper-Calvinist Universal Salvation

leads to the famous paradox that the ancient Greek philosopher Zeno discussed, called the Achilles paradox (also called, the dichotomy paradox, or the paradox of the racetrack), which shows how a person, if traveling through time by every number on any segment of the number line (if represented by the Real numbers) rather than by the integers only, cannot get from one point to the next through time, since a person has to traverse through infinite other points.[2] To get from any one time to the next, one can never complete the task of traveling through an unending set of time moments between the times: one never can complete the task of traveling through a set of moments through time sequentially if there is no end to the set of moments. The person therefore could not even move at all,[3] and they could never get from one point to the next. They could only be in absolute stillness. Instead of pulsating through time along the horizontal timeline, analogous to a person counting by integers, the person would be frozen in the alternate reality of being in one still moment, not moving through horizontal time at all. The only escape would be if the person were pulled out, plucked out, of that state, out of the infinity of moments, by a Being, a Power, that has the capacity to do so, brought back from annihilation and underworldly sleep. And we do see this sort of plucking out mentioned in Scripture in Zechariah 13:8–9; 9:11; Psalm 79:11; 16:10, and others. Also consider these:

> 11 I have overthrown some of you, as God overthrew Sodom and Gomorrah, and ye were as a firebrand plucked out of the burning: yet have ye not returned unto me, saith the LORD. 12 Therefore thus will I do unto thee, O Israel: and because I will do this unto thee, prepare to meet thy God, O Israel. (Amos 4:11–12)

> And the LORD said unto Satan, The Lord rebuke thee, O Satan; even the LORD that hath chosen Jerusalem rebuke thee: is not this a brand plucked out of the fire? (Zech 3:2)

> Because thou wilt not leave my soul in hell, neither wilt thou suffer thine Holy One to see corruption. (Acts 2:27)

GOD appears to remove and pluck beings out of the vertical underworld—which would mean GOD puts their consciousness and/or soul back

---

[2]. This involves a non-discrete model of space and time, where time moments resemble points the Real number line (R), where there are infinite quantities of infinite points (numbers) between any two non-identical points (numbers).

[3]. Dowden, "Zeno's Paradoxes," section 3.a.ii.

GOD Pulls Souls Out of the Vertical Infinity

into having mental contents, and into having conscious activity and self-existence. This is being pulled out of the *underworld*, including hell—and it is *not* referring to being pulled out of the Lake of Fire. Plucking out only happens pre-Eschaton, in the contexts of the underworlds, in Scripture, and it does not happen in the context of the Lake of Fire (GOD)—which one is, strictly speaking, seemingly *never* apart from, and *not* immersed in. This is a picture of GOD as *Savior*: the one who removes a person from the underworld state they are in. Therefore, in the systematic theology of Hyper-Calvinist universal salvation, a picture emerges of a Creator GOD who creates all beings *in order to save them*, and he does this via infinitely intense self-sacrifice and love (Heb 2:17), which is quite the inverse of the nonlogical cruel tyrant God of traditional Calvinism (non-universalist and non-scriptural Calvinism), who inexplicably creates staggering numbers of beings only to condemn and torture them unimaginably, forever.

The above Zenoic mathematical description may or may not align well with *actual* reality, and with what is happening in the infinite deepening of the vertical infinity time gap of the pre-Eschaton self-nonexistence that we are informed about in Scripture, but something like this sort of descending into the stillness of vertical infinity happens, where the self stills, into ceasing to exist, only an empty self and soul (if even that), without consciousness. Then the LORD brings back a new soul, one that is watched by GOD: when it is watched by GOD, it exists. Psalm 39:11–13, analyzed above, also is a passage about GOD again hearing us, as in Jonah. This is, at least in part, what reverses the annihilation and underworldly existence, Again, this illustrates the criticality in Scripture placed on a person being heard by GOD, where in Jonah 2, the hearing of GOD was during the annihilation, but from prayers that were from earlier, during the first life, in earthly physical existence.

In the time gap, the vertical infinity of pre-Eschaton self-nonexistence, a person is brought into stillness, sleep, and annihilation of self. Everything is different about the situation for the self, however, when it is brought back into existence in resurrection at the start of the Eschaton. Scripture makes it clear GOD is doing the removal of dormant the soul from the underworld existence (Ps 16:10). If the empty (devoid of self) soul continues to exist through the time of no mental content (self-nonexistence), it is GOD who awakens the person, bringing them mental content again (GOD is the only one who can create a mind, a spirit, and give it mental content, see Luke 11:39–40). There is nothing the human does to contribute to this resurrection, or to bring it about. It is done only by GOD, for all people, in two stages in the Eschaton, where he is solely responsible for making us who and what we are and will be—it is not the human and their supposed free will that creates (self-creates) the person:

> Know ye that the LORD he is God: it is he that hath made us, and not we ourselves; we are his people, and the sheep of his pasture.
> (Ps 100:3)

If we were to make ourselves (such as with our supposed free will), we would be self-creating, meaning that there is no external cause to our self, and thus the only entity that can cause the self is the self. This violates how GOD creates all things (Rev 4:11), including our inner minds (Luke 11:39–40), and it appears to be the inverse of what is said in Psalm 100:3. GOD could only create us as corrupt (as Adam and Eve were, which is why they sinned—discussed in a chapter below), wherein he had to destroy us, in order to re-create us as new, as we really are, at the Eschaton, so we can see him as he is. Since GOD is identical to love (1 John 4:7–8), and since GOD is infinite (Ps 145:7 KJV wording), then GOD is infinite love, and his bringing people from nonexistence all the way to salvation, can only be a production of infinite love.

18

GOD, Lake of Fire, is the Refiner's Fire

Recall that Isaiah 25:8 referred to death being *swallowed up* in victory. When we are *swallowed* by something, our earthly understanding is that we are *inside of* it. We are swallowed because the LORD is the *Consuming* Fire. The concept of being *inside of* GOD would appear to fit within the description of a consuming Lake of Fire swallowing, devouring, in his thorough immolating of all. The conclusion being discovered is: just as GOD is love, and therefore made of, composed of, love, GOD is also Fire, and therefore is made of, composed of, Fire, whatever the ineffable supernatural characteristics of that spiritual GOD-Fire are.

> For the LORD thy God is a consuming fire, even a jealous God. (Deut 4:24)
>
> For our God is a consuming fire. (Heb 12:29)

I believe it is self-evident that the "is" being used in each of these verses, regarding how he *is* the Consuming Fire, would be the "is" of identity (a = b), not the "is" of property possession ("the angel's garment *is* white"; that is, the garment has the property of being white, but is not identical to the color white). Therefore, I will work from the conclusion that the Consuming Fire (GOD, LORD, YHWH, Θεός) *is* Fire (Lake of Fire). And GOD being the Lake of Fire is, it seems, why GOD is called the "Consuming Fire" in Scripture: he consumes: swallows up (death and hell), brings all things into his Refiner's Fire, and therefore brings all things to an end (1 Pet 4:7; Mark 13:31), restoring all things (Acts 3:21), as he destroys the corrupted outer veneer of things, and makes new the *inside* (the spirit) of all things:

Hyper-Calvinist Universal Salvation

> 13 The LORD looketh from heaven; he beholdeth all the sons of men. 14 From the place of his habitation he looketh upon all the inhabitants of the earth. 15 He fashioneth their hearts alike; he considereth all their works. (Ps 33:13–15)

> Neither is there any creature that is not manifest in his sight: but all things are naked and opened unto the eyes of him with whom we have to do. (Heb 4:13)

> Thou hast set our iniquities before thee, our secret sins in the light of thy countenance. (Ps 90:8)

> Hell is naked before him, and destruction hath no covering. (Job 26:6)

> Hell and destruction are before the LORD: how much more then the hearts of the children of men? (Prov 15:11)

Humans are not identical to their bodies, but rather, the core of their being, their insides, is what they are: since GOD is a spirit, and we are in that Image, therefore we are spirit (see Eccl 12:7; John 1:9, 1:13, and 6:63): being a Spirit is the core of GOD, and thus his identity, so if there is anything about GOD we must be in the image of, it is that we are also each spirits, at the core of our being. GOD is also an innerness: he is his inner Fire, the center of his Being:

> Out of heaven he made thee to hear his voice, that he might instruct thee: and upon earth he shewed thee his great fire; and thou heardest his words *out of the midst of the fire*. (Deut 4:36)

The voice of the Consuming Fire (GOD) comes out from within himself, from the midst of himself, where "midst" indicates the core, an innermostnesst—as if referring to the deepest innermostness of the Fire. Speaking comes from the innermost core of a person:

> Out of the abundance of the heart the mouth speaketh. (Matt 12:34)

GOD speaks from the heart, and therefore from the *midst* (innermost core), and speaking happens from the heart, which means from the core, the deep inner regions, from the inner spirit of a person. Therefore, we should expect to find verses in Scripture referring to GOD speaking from *deep* within himself, from the center of his Fire, from deep within his fiery Being.

For these reasons, the reality of GOD, who is Consuming Fire, is more like our *inner* selves, and it is from this *inner* core, the deep center

GOD, Lake of Fire, is the Refiner's Fire

of ourselves, that GOD interacts with us (1 Sam 16:7). The Fire of GOD, therefore, will be visible to consume and immolate the earth at the Eschaton, but when we speak of GOD igniting, or burning, the earth already *now* (2 Pet 3:7; John 5:25), in a less fully revealed way now, it indicates that GOD is burning people from the inside, from their soul and spirit, in addition to burning the earth. GOD is a Fire that speaks from deep *within*, "out of the *midst* the fire" (Deut 4:36), and as he speaks from deep within himself, his innermostness interacts with our innermostness. And since he is Fire, and since he is interacting with our innermostness, that would indicate that the deepest part of our being is *touching*, and inside of, GOD's Fire, *now*. And we know GOD (Christ) has this interaction with *all* people, *now*, as discussed above when we discussed John 12:32. GOD "was the true Light, which lighteth every man that cometh into the world" (John 1:9). So, in summary, GOD is supernatural Consuming Fire that is everywhere, appearing locally in specific places at times, and always speaking from his innermost.

There are many references in the Old Testament to GOD being Fire (Consuming Fire), and to the Eschaton Fire/Lake of Fire. Consider these:

> 4 The LORD talked with you face to face in the mount out of the *midst* of the fire, 5 (I stood between the LORD and you at that time, to shew you the word of the LORD: for ye were afraid by reason of the fire, and went not up into the mount;) saying, 6 I am the LORD thy God, which brought thee out of the land of Egypt, from the house of bondage. (Deut 5:4–6)

> 22 These words the LORD spake unto all your assembly in the mount out of the *midst* of the fire, of the cloud, and of the thick darkness, with a great voice: and he added no more. And he wrote them in two tables of stone, and delivered them unto me. 23 And it came to pass, when ye heard the voice out of the midst of the darkness, (for the mountain did burn with fire,) that ye came near unto me, even all the heads of your tribes, and your elders; 24 And ye said, Behold, the LORD our God hath shewed us his glory and his greatness, and we have heard his voice out of the *midst* of the fire: we have seen this day that God doth talk with man, and he liveth. 25 Now therefore why should we die? for *this great fire will consume us*: if we hear the voice of the LORD our God any more, then we shall die. 26 For who is there of all flesh, that hath heard the voice of the living God speaking out of the *midst* of the fire, as we have, and lived? 27 Go thou near, and hear all that the LORD our God shall say: and speak thou unto us all that the LORD our

Hyper-Calvinist Universal Salvation

> God shall speak unto thee; and we will hear it, and do it. 28 And the LORD heard the voice of your words, when ye spake unto me; and the LORD said unto me, I have heard the voice of the words of this people, which they have spoken unto thee: they have well said all that they have spoken. (Deut 5:22–28)

GOD is acting in our souls, our spirits. Other people cannot be in our innermost self and soul, but GOD can, and is: he is always in our innermostness (Eph 1:23 and 4:6). For that reason, and since apart from Christ we can do nothing (John 15:5), if we are to be purified now, only GOD can do it within us. And GOD's Fire, lighting all people from within (John 1:9), interacting with all people, can therefore only be purifying all people, since GOD is the Fire of *purification* (see Mal 3:3, which is cited below). The logic of this sequence of ideas leads directly to the conclusion that the Lake of Fire, this innermost Fire that is GOD, the Lake of Fire, Fire-Eschaton, Consuming Fire, is *also* the *Refiner's Fire* mentioned in the Old and New Testaments. The Refiner's Fire is fully revealed at the Eschaton (Mal 3:1–3; Zech 13:9), but *also* is refining us *now* and in the past (see Isa 48:9–11; Ps 66:10–12), just as GOD, the Consuming Fire, is fully revealed at the Eschaton, and through a glass darkly before that time (1 Cor 13:12). GOD is a Fire that is always igniting our souls, always acting in our insides, creating our insides (Luke 11:39–40). The Refiner's Fire is a Fire that cleans a person, like *soap*, which is the work of GOD, not of man. The Lake of Fire at the Eschaton is therefore a *baptism*, a *soap*, that saves, cleans, both saved and condemned.

> 1 Behold, I will send my messenger, and he shall prepare the way before me: and the Lord, whom ye seek, shall suddenly come to his temple, even the messenger of the covenant, whom ye delight in: behold, he shall come, saith the LORD of hosts. 2 But who may abide *the day of his coming*? and who shall stand when he appeareth? for *he is like a refiner's fire, and like fullers' soap*: 3 and *he shall sit as a refiner and purifier of silver*: and he *shall purify the sons of Levi*, and *purge them* as gold and silver, that they may offer unto the LORD an offering in righteousness. (Mal 3:1–3)

As with Numbers 31:23, Malachi 3:1–3 is also future-pointing. Note again the anticipation of the fire in the future in Malachi 3:1–3, talking about GOD cleansing the sinners with Fire at the end of all things ("the day of his coming"), when he is revealed. These are the same properties as with Lake of Fire/Eschaton Fire, so the Refiner's Fire is also a reference to this

GOD, Lake of Fire, is the Refiner's Fire

Fire at the Eschaton (GOD) that saves all the unchosen. And considering the Refiner's Fire as a baptism in GOD-Christ, the Eschaton being a Fire baptism would appear to link together the following two future-pointing Fire baptism verses:

> John answered, saying unto them all, I indeed baptize you with water; but one mightier than I cometh, the latchet of whose shoes I am not worthy to unloose: he *shall* baptize you with the Holy Ghost and with fire . . . (Luke 3:16)

> I indeed baptize you with water unto repentance: but he that cometh after me is mightier than I, whose shoes I am not worthy to bear: he *shall* baptize you with the Holy Ghost, and with fire . . . (Matt 3:11)

The destiny of a human, therefore, is Fire baptism, which will be fully revealed at the Eschaton.

It is important to spell out the scriptural evidence that Refiner's Fire = YHWH/Θεός, so that we can be sure we have not made an error in our analysis, and further, since many scholars may doubt that Refiner's Fire = YHWH/Θεός. Above we stated we know that the Refiner's Fire is GOD since the Refiner's Fire is soap (Mal 3:2), that which cleanses, and since the Fire of GOD *also* is the cleanser of the soul—the *only* Being that can cleanse the soul. Consider this future-pointing passage from the Old Testament law, but also about the purification of the Eschaton Fire:[1]

---

1. Numbers 31 is written in present tense, except for verses 22–24, which are in future tense, and which are the verses about the washing and the Refiner's Fire. So, in that part of the passage, the fieriness and washing has a future element to it, whereas the rest of the passage about the goings on of the day. Also, and as an aside, Numbers 31 contains passages of surprising and bizarre "laws," such as verse 17: "Now therefore kill every male among the little ones, and kill every woman that hath known man by lying with him." But this is a passage about what *Moses* said, *not* what the LORD said, and therefore, it is not GOD's law. The Bible is written by GOD, but there are many places where it contains account of humans speaking to each other, and often those passages contain human folly. I often have atheists telling me the Bible is absurd because of these passages about GOD's laws, but I tell them they need to read the passage more carefully, and that these passages are about men speaking to each other (see verse 15, where it says "Moses said unto them") in Scripture, and where GOD reveals the absurdity of man's thinking (see Rom 3:4; Ps 116:11; 1 Cor 1:21). But then in verse 21, the voice changes to being GOD's voice, the ineffable, beyond-what-can-be-understood, all-caps Tetragrammaton: "This is the ordinance of the law which the LORD commanded Moses." And from that point, the passage goes directly into discussion of the purifying Fire. Another part of the Bible that exhibits this contrast of men talking to one another compared to GOD speaking is Exodus 20–21. In Exodus 20 we are told GOD is speaking, and then we are given the

Hyper-Calvinist Universal Salvation

> ...every thing that may abide the fire, ye *shall make it go through the fire*, and *it shall be clean*: nevertheless it *shall* be purified with the water of separation: and all that abideth not the fire ye *shall* make go through the water. (Num 31:23)

Understanding the deep mechanics of how GOD's Fire is interacting with humanity, washing the person in their innermost being, appears to give information about how GOD saves humanity by his Fire, both in the past, now, and at the future Eschaton. Having direct contact with GOD in his innermost being reveals the awareness of the presence of GOD (feeling him, being one with his Being, etc.) deep within all people now. The Refiner's Fire is igniting the world now, and at all times of the world's existence, where reality exists in a state of imminent immolation in Christ, as if always on the verge of total ignition, explosion, in GOD.

Scripture also contains passages about humans being saved *in* the Eschaton Fire, inside of it, perhaps in its *midst*, its center, at the core of GOD. Consider the following revealing passage, about every sinner, which is every person:

> 6 Howl ye; for the *day of the LORD is at hand*; it shall come as a destruction from the Almighty. 7 Therefore shall all hands be faint, and *every man's heart shall melt*: 8 and they shall be afraid: pangs and sorrows shall take hold of them; they shall be in pain as a woman that travaileth:[2] *they shall be amazed one at another; their faces shall be as*[3] *flames.* 9 Behold, the day of the LORD cometh, cruel both with wrath and fierce anger, to lay the land desolate: and he shall destroy the sinners thereof out of it. (Isa 13:6–9)

We know that this passage is about the Eschaton, since (i) it is the time of the birth pangs (seemingly at the peak of them), and since (ii) in the passage,

---

Ten Commandments. But in Exodus 21 we are told in verse 1 that this is an account of humans speaking to one another, wherein more absurdity springs forth, in discussion of an eye for an eye (21:24).

2. This travailing in pain (birth panges) is one of the main reasons this passage is about the Eschaton, in addition to also possibly being about historical events from the Old Testament times.

3. Note that it says "as" flames. Above we have noted that GOD's fire is a spiritual fire, and therefore will not be identical to ordinary physical fire, which is a plasma state of matter. I believe this is why Isaiah 13:8 says their faces will be "as" fire, since apparently GOD's Fire is like enough to physical fire that it is labeled as "fire" in Scripture, but then again, GOD's Fire is not an identical match to physical fire (corrupted), where GOD's Fire, being uncorrupted, and unlike the ordinary physical fire of the fallen (corrupted) physical world, is the Fire of salvation.

GOD, Lake of Fire, is the Refiner's Fire

all people are on fire, as if there is fire everywhere (Lake of Fire), where they are melting, rather than burning, as if it is a different sort of Fire, and where people are nevertheless in a state of amazement (rather than torment), apparently when looking at each other aflame. The mental state of amazement implies an absence of torment (such as torment from being engulfed in fire), since such a level of torment would, seemingly, obliterate amazement from being in the immediate continuousness. This passage reveals that the day of the LORD involves defining the word "day" like an epoch ("back in the day"), not a twenty-four-hour period. It is a time when GOD's Eschaton birth pangs increase in intensity through time, into the Eschaton (since, by definition, birth pangs intensify). And as we can see, Isaiah 13:6 reveals that the day was *at hand* at the time of the writing of Isaiah, deep into the Old Testament times. In the passage, we find that the day of the LORD, an event of Fire, involves *amazement* in *all* people over their faces being fully immolated and/or transformed into fieriness (verse 8). This is for all people, since verse 7 says "every man's heart . . . ," indicating it is written about all people, with the subject unchanging into verse 8. Having amazement in being immolated seems only a state of consciousness that could be imputed into a person by the one who has capacity to put amazement into the mind of a human, who is a Being of Fire: the supernatural Creator. Apparently all people have been in his Eschaton Lake of Fire by that point, and have been changed, to have mental states difficult for us to understand on this side of time (on this side of the Eschaton). These are states only GOD can invoke, describing the specific transitioning he produces in bringing the unchosen to being fully salvific amid the Eschaton Fire.

Isaiah 13:6–9 begins by describing itself as *destruction from GOD*, and as the day of the LORD (verse 6), indicating that this is an Eschaton-level situation, since it affects all people (verse 7): one of the many Old Testament references to the Eschaton Fire event, the Lake of Fire (Baptism in GOD): the immolation from within, inside of, the ocean of the Consuming Fire. At verse 7, *all* hearts melt in this day. In verse 8, we see a transition point has occurred, *into amazement*, after the terror and difficulty of the pre-Eschaton birth contractions (Matt 24:7–8; Isa 13:8–9[4]) leading into

---

4. 13:8 is in the context of the Eschaton due to verse six, where they are anticipating the day of destruction, the day of the LORD. Then verse seven involves the biblical concept of the world melting, and people's hearts melting, where the melting in verse eight is from their being in fire, where first it is terror, and then amazement. And in verse nine, this is all brought into the Eschaton concept of the day of *wrath*, the day that he destroys the sinners, just as all of us will be annihilated, and later destroyed from being flesh

Hyper-Calvinist Universal Salvation

the Eschaton. Though it has been missed by theologians and pastors for centuries, and since the early church, Scripture is direct in saying that all are saved *by Fire*. In Isaiah 13:8, we are told of those in the Lake of Fire that their faces "shall be as flames." This appears to say that in this Eschaton event, faces *are* fire, rather than *on* fire. This appears to be after our hearts have already melted. But if our hearts have melted, then so have our faces—but verse 8 tells us that the faces *still exist*. By this point, there cannot be any flesh left, so they would only be fire—hence, their faces shall be as flames: faces of nonphysical fire. Whatever is going on at this point, we know that in some way the person is made out of fire, of some sort, in some way, at the time of the Lake of Fire revealing. There is discussion in Scripture of this future time when the flesh is destroyed and the Spirit is saved; for example, consider again:

> 4 in the name of our Lord Jesus Christ, when ye are gathered together, and my spirit, with the power of our Lord Jesus Christ, 5 to deliver such an one unto Satan for the destruction of the flesh, that the spirit may be saved in the day of the Lord Jesus. (1 Cor 5:4–5)

These events happen at the tail end of the day of LORD (which would be the Eschaton), since flesh of the man will be entirely *destroyed*, at the first death, when the physical body we presently have is destroyed in the grave. The person has a body that's been brought back at the first resurrection, and thus the flesh has not yet been destroyed. So, the destruction event of 1 Corinthians 5:5 can only be the Eschaton Fire, the Lake of Fire, which occurs after the descension of Christ at the Eschaton.

(discussed in later chapters), and will be destroyed as sinners, since we are all sinners. I believe Isa 13:8 involves the concept that the Lake of Fire almost "forces," for lack of better words, the unchosen into repentance at the fire-Eschaton for the unchosen. Look at how the verse transitions midway through it. The verse starts off with a reference to the birth pangs, and therefore the Eschaton. It is mentioned that they have screaming pain, like a woman in birth labor, apparently at the end of the pangs (that is, at the Eschaton), and we find out they are being immolated. So, they are in the midst of the Fire-Eschaton (GOD); but notice that after their mention of travailing in painful horror, *they* are *amazed*. And they are amazed at one another, possibly because they are all in Fire. I believe amazement is not a state of mind one can be in if one is in screaming pain. I believe a woman at the peak of birth pains will tell you that the only thing in the consciousness at that point was the ineffable terror of the pain, and amazement was absent from the consciousness. Therefore, there seems to be a shift mid-verse, where the immolated people went *from* screaming terror *to* amazement, which would indicate the salvation "process" carrying forth, during the Eschaton GOD-fire.

GOD, Lake of Fire, is the Refiner's Fire

So, at the Lake of Eschaton Fire (YHWH, Christ, GOD, Θεός), our bodies melt and we become fire beings of some sort, angels of holy fire (Heb 1:7; Matt 22:30; Luke 20:36 in KJV wording), by the melting of our resurrected bodies (first resurrection), in the Lake of Fire. Consider the following:

> 12 Now if any man build upon this foundation gold, silver, precious stones, wood, hay, stubble; 13 every man's work shall be made manifest: for *the day shall declare it*, because it shall be *revealed by fire*; and the fire shall try every man's work of what sort it is. 14 If any man's work abide which he hath built thereupon, he shall receive a reward. 15 If any man's work shall be burned, he shall suffer loss: *but he himself shall be saved; yet so as by fire*. (1 Cor 3:12–15)

If we look carefully at this passage, we see something that tells us that the Lake of Fire *is* the *washing* event, the baptism-of-Fire event of the Eschaton. The Lake of Fire, which is what this passage is referring to, exposes the faith (and works) of the person, and burns away that which is combustible in GOD's Fire (1 Cor 15:50). That is the cleansing. So, the baptism of Fire is the purpose of the Lake of Fire: remove the flesh, and preserve (salt) the spirit. Here are more verses that appear to be about the Lake of Fire as the baptism of Fire.

> Behold, *I have refined thee*, but not with silver; *I have chosen thee in the furnace* of affliction. (Isa 48:10)

> And it shall come to pass, that in all the land, saith the LORD, two parts therein shall be cut off and die; but the third shall be left therein. And *I will bring the third part through the fire, and will refine them as silver is refined, and will try them as gold is tried: they shall call on my name*, and I will hear them: I will say, It is my people: and they shall say, The LORD is my God. (Zech 13:8–9)

> But the wicked shall perish, and the enemies of the LORD shall be as the fat of lambs: they shall *consume; into smoke* shall they *consume* away. (Ps 37:20)

> For a fire is kindled in mine anger, and shall burn unto the lowest hell, and shall consume the earth with her increase, and set on fire the foundations of the mountains… They shall be burnt with hunger, and devoured with burning heat, and with bitter destruction: I will also send the teeth of beasts upon them, with the poison of serpents of the dust. (Deut 32:22)

19

All People Are Christ's Body, Omnitemporally Drawn to Him

THIS CHAPTER FOLLOWS CLOSELY from the previous chapter. In the previous chapter, we found how GOD is a deep presence, directly known within, that baptizes and cleanses with his Fire. In this chapter, we will discuss the plainspoken scriptural evidence that GOD is given to all people, and all people are the body of Christ. Typically, I hear it stated that it is among the visible church, and in the church buildings, where the saved people are, and which is the body of Christ, but the scriptural account is that *all* people, all temples, are Christ's body. Consider this pointed, but little discussed, verse:

> Where there is neither Greek nor Jew, circumcision nor uncircumcision, Barbarian, Scythian, bond nor free: but *Christ is all, and in all*.[1] (Col 3:11)

This verse would appear to be plainest of verification that the body of Christ *is all people*, not *some* people. Since GOD knows people at all times, and he knows our true self, which is the self that is looking at him (1 John 3:2),

---

1. Note that this verse says *both* that Christ *is* all, and then immediately after, is *in* all. So, GOD has *to be* us, and also be *in* us. This tells us that "Christ is all" does not mean something like this: "I am GOD." The full view of this passage reveals that we are *in* him (and thus we are not mathematically *identical to* him, where his haecceity and qualia are indistinguishable from our haecceity and qualia), but also we *are* him, so in some ways, sharing in his existence, participating in his divinity (2 Pet 1:4). This reveals how close humans, all people, actually *are* to GOD, whether they are aware of this or not. A person's being, their identity, soul, is inside of GOD:

> There is neither Jew nor Greek, there is neither bond nor free, there is neither male nor female: for ye are *all one in Christ Jesus*. (Gal 3:28)

All People Are Christ's Body, Omnitemporally Drawn to Him

GOD therefore always knows a person in their saved state. The old sinner is present during this time in the physical reality, but GOD can also see in their existence how they are beings that were created to see him directly after the fiery trial of their lives (1 Pet 4:12–14), when the trouble of the physical existence (John 16:33) is completed.

The tongues-of-fire passage in Acts 2 is the commencement of the promised Holy Ghost Fire baptism, and note that it did not happen until after Jesus ascended. So, we know that what is being spoken of in Luke 3:16 and Matthew 3:11 is prophecy of future events *after* his ascension. After the tongues-of-fire event, Holy Spirit baptism was discussed in the present tense, as seen in the following stirring and starkly universalist (universal salvation) and even Hyper-Calvinist passage:

> 11 but all these worketh that one and the selfsame Spirit, dividing to *every man* severally as he will. 12 For as the body is one, and hath many members, and all the members of that one body, being many, are one body: so also is Christ. 13 For by one Spirit *are we all baptized into one body*, whether we be Jews or Gentiles, whether we be bond or free; and *have been all made to drink into one Spirit*. (1 Cor 12:11–13)

This passage appears to say that all people *are* the body of Christ, not just present believers. GOD is one, and thus his body (people) is also, wherein all people now, whether they know it or not, are one (also see Phil 2:2).

From what I have seen in my life, Christians typically seem to believe that it is the pure who are his body, not the impure, but that cannot be correct since we are all sinners, and the Bible has a very different view about who is the body:

> And those members of the body, which we think to be less honourable, upon these we bestow more abundant honour; and our uncomely parts have more abundant comeliness. (1 Cor 12:23)

As I have eluded to at various places in this book, there is a sort of breakthrough in how one views a person when one has a Hyper-Calvinist universal salvation theology in their theological framework. If GOD is aware of us all times, which he would have to be, since he is omniscient, then he knows us at all stages of our existence:

1. With him before time (Eccl 12:7), and inside of him before time (inside of him since we are *born of* him, see John 1:13).

Hyper-Calvinist Universal Salvation

2. As living souls (Gen 2:7), meaning our time as creatures who are put into the physical dimension, made to believe they are identical to their biological bodies (Eccl 3:11).

3. Vanishing into annihilation and the sleep of self-nonexistence after physical body death, and up to the point of the pre-salvific first resurrection, during the earlier stages and intensities of the Eschaton.

4. Salvation at the descending of Christ after the first resurrection, into the infinity of afterlife in GOD's Being.

GOD knows us fully at each of these times. We know that some aspects of stage 2 are blotted out of existence, since GOD blots out our sins from existence (see Isa 43:25; 1 John 2:2; and Mark 3:28 in KJV wording only), but the point is that if GOD sees us, and knows us, as all of these, but as arriving and being our *real self* (1 John 3:2) when at Eschaton salvation (stage 4), then all these stages of a person are real, from our vantagepoint now, in stage 2. So, people now, in stage 2, whether condemned or saved in the present, are also taking part in stage 4, and being saved by GOD. But if all people are *being* saved *now*, then they are being pulled to, drawn to, GOD now (John 12:32). This interaction with GOD to all people was in full form by the time of the ascension (see John 12:32) and completes at the Eschaton's first resurrection (see John 6:44). But note that this indicates that all people today are interacting with GOD, due to being drawn to him, being pulled to him, where they will be pulled into his Eschaton Fire (Lake of Fire). When I am doing ministry inside of the jail during my day-to-day work, I look at the men not only as needing Jesus today, but also that even the unsaved will experience—often unbeknownst to them—deepening in Christ, and an increase in closeness to him day after day, such as, to give one example, by groaning and agonizing more deeply from one day to the next over the complete emptiness of not being indwelt by Christ-GOD, and thus having the inner need for oneness with the LORD (Heb 2:11) deepen from day to day, bringing the person closer and closer to crying out to their Savior. In this context, the realization has been put into me, in my workaday life, to call any person who might be condemned, "brother."

Consider again this passage, but the fire baptism being future:

> I indeed baptize you with water unto repentance: but he that cometh after me is mightier than I, whose shoes I am not worthy to bear: *he shall baptize* you with the Holy Ghost, *and with fire*. (Matt 3:11)

All People Are Christ's Body, Omnitemporally Drawn to Him

As just noted, in John 12:32, Jesus tells us that he was drawing all men to himself at least by the time of the ascension.

> And I, if I be lifted up from the earth, will draw all men unto me. (John 12:32)

So, the idea is that Christ is pulling all people to himself today, and more[2] the next day, into the Eschaton, always drawing and pulling us closer.

The future-pointing verses of Luke 3:16 and Matthew 3:11 (cited above) are written to all people, due to the fact that the gospel is to be preached to every creature (Mark 16:15). So, the baptism of Fire, which is happening now through a glass darkly, and is fully revealed at the Eschaton, where by that time all have been salted (cleansed, baptized) with Fire (Mk 9:49), is so decisive and of GOD's infinite power, that it burns past any sin.

> And I heard as it were the voice of a great multitude, and as the voice of many waters, and as the voice of mighty thunderings, saying, Alleluia: for the Lord God omnipotent reigneth. (Rev 19:6)

This Fire baptism appears to offer explanation for how those who are unchosen, and who are of Satan, can be definitively but inexplicably *saved* at the day of the LORD (which is the Eschaton Fire, at full revealing, and in pulling all things to it before the full revealing). Consider the following:

> To deliver such an one unto Satan for the destruction of the flesh, that the spirit may be saved in the day of the Lord Jesus. (1 Cor 5:5)

This "destruction" of the flesh would have to be via the Fire-Eschaton (day of the LORD Jesus)—at GOD's saving of all souls at the Eschaton—since this destruction of the flesh, and transformation of the Spirit, occurs at the end of all things[3] (Eschaton) for this unchosen and unsaved person,

---

2. The drawing GOD (Christ) does to humans can only *increase* through time. That is because GOD is a GOD of increase (Luke 17:5; Acts 6:7; Col 2:19; John 3:30), since he has the heart of infinite Love that can only overflow. If the overflow was not increasing, all through eternity and forever, then GOD's love would be either decreasing (which is not possible) or stagnant and incapable of growth (also not possible), increasing as his body and kingdom increases. GOD is constant (unchanging) increasing.

3. A second possible "entity" that is beyond thingness would be our innermost consciousness (soul). That innermostness is where GOD looks when he looks at us, it is where GOD lives, and it is in his image, and thus it must be also in the direction of being post-thingness. We are a spirit, as GOD is a Spirit (John 4:24). This does not necessarily mean that every thought we have in post-thingness; and we know that GOD is the Creator of our innerness (Luke 11:39–40). So there must a still center, a base, of our being, that ventures into post-thingness, wherein our conscious minds are thing, created

Hyper-Calvinist Universal Salvation

wherein it leads to salvation. First Corinthians 5:5 also reveals the two stages of salvation discussed above, and discussed again in more detail in the next chapter.

To speak informally for a moment, the concept that all sinners make up the body of Christ (GOD) may be an idea too radical for humans to generally accept or admit, and it is too philosophically explosive for humans to take in. I believe this concept, that Christ is all and in all, is at the core of the atoning work of the crucified GOD, and therefore can only be understood as mystery, the assurance of the Mystery (see Col 2:2), via a mindset of the infinite, to see into GOD's understanding, which is infinite (Ps 147:5 KJV wording).

---

by GOD, but deeper than that is a connection we have with the LORD that is more in his image, and is beyond being a thing, and which will survive when the end of all things is near—which includes the end of our minds being near (which is what is involved in the theology of annihilationism. So, this innermost area of mind would not be a created thing, but a created spirit: a created trans-thing.

20

Why GOD Created Humans With Sin and Pain

A New Solution to the Problem of Pain and Evil

THIS LATE CHAPTER COULD be the most important of this book. This chapter answers the following question:

> Why did GOD create humans to live in a world of pain, instead of creating them just to be immediately put into the glorious afterlife?

The answer to this, presented in this chapter, reveals why GOD created humans all as corrupt, wherein there is a need for an Eschaton omnisalvation of humanity. This is a variation of the famous problem of evil, also sometimes referred to as the problem of pain, which goes as follows:

> How can a perfect, uncorrupt, and infinitely loving GOD create a reality that is imperfect, corrupt, and full of pain and evil?

I realize that the typical answer (the pop theology answer) to this will be something like: because humans needed to choose GOD with their free will, but some didn't, so evil and pain entered the world. But since, as discussed earlier, there is no scripture that supports this sort of a view, and since GOD is the one who creates all things and thereby is in control of all things, the popular free will response to the problem of evil will not be considered in this book as a scriptural solution.

There are actually multiple ways to answer the problem of evil quite readily, but in this chapter, I will just focus on a strictly logical principle

Hyper-Calvinist Universal Salvation

from Scripture, which shows a spectacular solution to the problem of evil. The simplest way to state the solution is as follows:

> Since GOD is the only uncorrupt Being, anything he creates, that is distinct from himself, can only have some distinctions from GOD, and thus have different attributes, and therefore, can only be corrupt.

The simple logical point that GOD, when he creates anything, creates things that are *distinct* from himself, is a starkly overlooked issue in theology, and one that gives clear answers to some of the deepest theological matters. It reveals answers to what have been viewed for centuries as the biggest theological mysteries and puzzles, such as why there is pain, why there is evil, or how an all-loving God can create a creation that has sin and sinful creatures in it.

The argument I will present follows the reasoning of the following two passages:

> 42 So also is the resurrection of the dead. It is sown in corruption; it is raised in incorruption: 43 it is sown in dishonour; it is raised in glory: it is sown in weakness; it is raised in power: 44 it is sown a natural body; it is raised a spiritual body. (1 Cor 15:42-44).

Every person is created as corrupt, but later is raised in incorruption. And more broadly, everything is created as corrupted, but GOD will restore all things, reconciling all to himself:

> And, having made peace through the blood of his cross, by him to reconcile all things unto himself; by him, I say, whether they be things in earth, or things in heaven. (Col 1:20)

First Corinthians 15:42 contains something seemingly always overlooked in Christian theology, which is that it appears GOD created humans, and all other created things, as imperfect (corrupt), and that is the only way he can create them. And this dilemma, of GOD creating all things corrupted, is alleviated by the fact that GOD restores all things, by uniting and/or atoning himself with all created things (Acts 3:21). I hear people commonly say, "Adam and Eve were perfect," or, "The garden of Eden was perfect," but Genesis 1-3 does not make any such claims, and Scripture indicates a different scenario going on:

Why GOD Created Humans With Sin and Pain

> And the vessel that he made of clay was marred in the hand of the potter: so he made it again another vessel, as seemed good to the potter to make it. (Jer 18:4)

> Blessed is the man to whom the Lord will not impute sin. (Rom 4:8)

In the King James Version, there are two passages I know of that speak of men being perfect (Job 1:1; Gen 6:9), but Scripture would explain that being due to GOD doing their works through such perfect men (see Isa 26:12; John 15:5), wherein sin was avoided because there was fear of the LORD. I believe Scripture would indicate these men were described as perfect because of GOD's working in them (Phil 1:6), but overall, the men inhabited corrupted flesh that was created by GOD, and would be made incorruptible not until the last day, as the previous chapters would indicate.

So, evil and pain are in the world because GOD created the world as corrupted, as that is the only way he can create. (This does not limit his omnipotence, because to create something distinct from himself that is not corrupted would involve contradiction, and therefore, impossibility. But to GOD, all is possible, not impossible: nothing is impossible with him—in other words, for GOD, there are not any impossible entities; they do not exist, so, all of what is real/possible exists for him.) Again, this is because he is the only noncorrupt entity, and therefore, what he creates will be corrupted. So, in answer to the key question, *why won't God stop the misery, the pain, the bloodshed, the poverty, the horror all over the world?* (problem of evil), the following argument offers an answer, from pure logic:

1. GOD is incorrupt.
2. There can only be one incorrupt entity.[1]
3. If GOD creates anything *distinct from* himself, it can only be corrupt:[2] GOD only creates corrupt entities.[3]

---

1. This is because if there were, for sake of argument, *two* incorrupt entities that were *distinct* in their incorruptness, one could only be less corrupt than the other, lest they have identical incorruptness. So, *ipso facto*, there can only be *one* incorrupt entity in all reality, in all possible worlds. This one incorrupt entity is, by definition, and by the pure logic of this reasoning, GOD. GOD is incorrupt, and all humans he creates are corrupt (1 Cor 15:42). All beings and entities and minds he creates are only corrupt.

2. This would be true even if what GOD creates is good, as our universe was at the point of creation (Genesis 1).

3. This does not mean that every conscious entity created will be sinful. If corruptness is related to evil, for any conscious entity (human being, etc.), there could be cases

Hyper-Calvinist Universal Salvation

4. What is corrupt has properties in violation with GOD's ways.
5. Beings created by GOD can only be of corruption (until restored at the time of salvation), some of whom will violate GOD's ways.
6. That leads to evil and sin (1 John 3:4).
7. Sin will lead to pain.

Therefore, GOD can only create corrupt beings, who will inevitably live in evil and pain. This is reversed when GOD restores all things. From this argument, we know that all realities need to be restored by GOD, as he has indicated he will for us in ours.

Sin and evil, in Scripture, are not identical. We know this because GOD creates evil, but does not create sin:

> But if, while we seek to be justified by Christ, we ourselves also are found sinners, is therefore Christ the minister of sin? God forbid. (Gal 2:17)

> I form the light, and create darkness: I make peace, and create evil: I the LORD do all these things. (Isa 45:7)

Since GOD creates all things, then sin must not be a thing. This would appear to indicate that sin is a void, a hole of nonbeing, a gap of nothingness in reality, that exists in the human soul (see Gal 6:3). Humans are a vessel, and the vessel, I propose, has aspects of it that are not yet created, deep within—they are pure void, nonbeing, nothingness. It is this that is involved in corruption, and it is that involves human sin in the soul. It is, I imagine, like a hole in the forest-floor that one does not see, but which one falls into and is hurt by. Does the hole exist? It could be argued that the hole does not exist, and it is just an arrangement of the contours of the land, and the hole is just our point of view, our way of looking at the contours of the land. So, something that does not exist led to the injury. That would amount to asserting that nothingness (that which is not created) caused the injury of the human. This nothingness in the soul—the hole in the soul, its regions that have not been created yet—is why humans sin.

---

where conscious beings GOD creates are corrupted but will not sin—since sin and evil are not identical (see below in this chapter for explanation). Perhaps some angels are created that are souls that are corrupted to a degree that sin is not a possibility for them. And perhaps we human beings who were put in this physical reality were beings *only* capable of sin, and that is why GOD put human beings in this physical reality, a trial, to bring us to sin in order to sacrifice his life for us via infinite love (discussed below), saving us at our deepest need, as sinners, expressing his perfect and infinite sacrifice and love.

Why GOD Created Humans With Sin and Pain

The following verse also uses the word "vessel" to define a human:

> And the vessel that he made of clay was marred in the hand of the potter: so he made it again another vessel, as seemed good to the potter to make it. (Jer 18:4)

So, let's look at that word "marred." That is the Hebrew word תָחַשׁ, or *sha-chath* (phonetic: shaw-khath'), and it means the following: "marred," "to go to ruin," "spoiled," "destroyed," "corrupted," "perishing," "ruined," "damaged," "injured," "to act corruptly," "of the pit." All these words of course designate imperfection, but also, these words are related to sin, especially like the words like "perishing," "injured," "corrupted," and "damaged." So, GOD created us marred, and a vessel, and that means we have an uncreated hole, a void, within us (in our souls). From the start, we had sin, but GOD did not create the sin, because the hole, the sin, is not a thing, and thus not a thing created, so it is a hole of nothingness. So, we were created as imperfect sinners, but GOD did not create the sin, since he is not the author of sin (Gal 2:17). So, Jesus, the LOGOS, is the Creator of all things, but *not* the author or creator of sin; therefore, sin is not a thing, it is no-thing. This hole in the soul can explain all the pain of the humans of the world.

And I think this is the key point of this chapter: If GOD creates humans as corrupted, since that is the only way he can create humans, then humans can only be disobedient, since they do not know GOD's ways, and they can only inevitably be sinful. And therefore, the only way GOD can interact with humans initially (pre-Eschaton), before his restoration of them is complete, *is in interacting with them as sinners* (since they are all sinners). So, GOD, who is in control, and creates all things, can only continuously create and interact with humans while they are sinners, and he can only save us in that state (Rom 5:6–8). This is why GOD sustains a world of evil and the scars of sin, until he restores what is corrupted, in whatever ways and timing he uses to do so.

We can start to see how it can be that there is sin in a reality created by GOD, but where GOD does not involve or create sin. Consider the first sin in our reality, the sin of Satan's in the garden, at the start of creation:

> Thine heart was lifted up because of thy beauty, thou hast corrupted thy wisdom by reason of thy brightness: I will cast thee to the ground, I will lay thee before kings, that they may behold thee. (Ezek 28:17)

Hyper-Calvinist Universal Salvation

The issue at hand is the mention in Ezekiel 28:17 of how Satan's eyes, his thoughts, his concentration, his view, went away from the LORD and onto his own body, wherein he noted his own appearance and concluded (reasoned) that it was beautiful. Apparently, his ruminations about himself lifted himself up, where in not looking at GOD—because he was looking at himself—he sinned (see Rom 14:23). So, all through this, GOD is in control, and sustains all things, but Satan has a corrupted soul, and only can act corrupted, so if GOD wants to keep him in existence, he only can by perpetuating the existence of a sinner. The same is true of every human being. If they are to exist, they will be created and sustained by GOD, where GOD has to therefore create and sustain a creature of corruption and sin. But the sin is not in GOD, or of GOD; it is a void in Satan's soul, an uncreated part, all through this transition. Thus, GOD does not create the sin, nor do the sin, but nevertheless, Satan is ruled by sin.

Some might ask the question: why would GOD not save humans, restore them, right after he created them, or perhaps a few moments after, to avoid their having to go through all the pain, atrocity, and misery of pre-Eschaton existence? The answer to that can only be because of GOD's infinite love: he will only operate by infinite love, and therefore, he had to use the cross to save, by being the infinite sacrifice, which is the expression of infinite love. So, humans had to live in a world of corruption in order to be saved from it by being made one with their Creator. I do not know how that can happen other than via infinite love, and therefore, via the cross, which is the act of infinite love:

> Greater love hath no man than this, that a man lay down his life for his friends. (John 15:13)

> 1 Blessed is he whose transgression is forgiven, whose sin is covered. 2 Blessed is the man unto whom the Lord imputeth not iniquity, and in whose spirit there is no guile. (Ps 32:1–2)

> Then God sent an evil spirit between Abimelech and the men of Shechem; and the men of Shechem dealt treacherously with Abimelech. (Judg 9:23)

Also see 1 Samuel 16:14–16 and Isaiah 19:13–14.

21

The Hour Is Coming, and Now Is

John 5:25 says, "Verily, verily, I say unto you, The hour is coming, and now is, when the dead shall hear the voice of the Son of God." This verse indicates that the Eschaton is coming, and is here now. In previous chapters, we touched on how the Eschaton is like an end-of-the-world event that is pulling all of creation at all times to it, as if reaching across time. But the omnipresent GOD is the Consuming Eschaton Fire, so we have to consider, just as John 5:25 says, that the Eschaton Fire is present at all times. Second Peter 3:7–8, discussed above, may also have a relation to these verses, in discussing how our world we live in and see every day has its purpose as being reserved for Fire, which I interpret to mean its purpose is to be immolated by the Lake of Fire and therein restored. It is as if the Fire of the Eschaton, being an Eschaton event, is also reaching to us from the future *now*, in some way, such as in that the earth is *both* being burned with Fire now, *and* at all pre-Eschaton times, but also will be *fully* immolated after Jesus is revealed in the Eschaton (appearing from within anomalous cloud-cover everywhere). (See Isa 65:24 for another interesting referenced to backward causation—cause happening before effect in time—used by GOD, in answering prayers before they are prayed.) The Fire of the Eschaton does not bring pain to the chosen (see Rev 2:11; 20:6). John 12:32 could hint at more information on this concept that the Lake of Fire is fully revealed at the Eschaton, but is, however, also present in the world now, its presence being active but not fully visible, not yet fully revealed, in the world leading into the Eschaton. This Fire, pulling us into the future, the fire of GOD, would appear to be the shaper of all of reality, all of history, being in all things (Eph 1:23), and pulling all things to the Eschaton restoration (Acts 3:21).

Hyper-Calvinist Universal Salvation

Scripture is quite specific that, on the one hand, what we are calling the Eschaton is a world-ending event at the end of time, leading into the end of all things (see 1 Pet 4:7), but also on the other hand, the Eschaton event is in fact *here now*, before the end of the world. Look at how John 5:25 is worded:

> Verily, verily, I say unto you, The hour is coming, and now is, when the dead shall hear the voice of the Son of God: and they that hear shall live. (John 5:25)

Further note that in Isaiah 26:20, where it appears that the Eschaton could start *earlier* than the end of the world (if we define the "end of the world" as the time of the splitting of the sky [see Luke 20:34–36] to the end of all things [1 Pet 4:7]), some are taken into a place to be with the Creator, before or during the time of the wrath (presumably this is the time of the great tribulation). This would seem to demonstrate that the Eschaton does not start in the same way or at the same chronological point for all people, and that there could be a start to Eschaton events for some, for those who escape the wrath.

So, it seems we need to expand the concept of the Eschaton into two parts, which is what we will find Scripture doing, and as we have already seen in both John 5:25, just cited, and Isaiah 26:20, just cited: there is a *final Eschaton*, involving the sky splitting, all flesh seeing GOD directly (Rev 1:7; Isa 40:5; Luke 3:6; 1 John 3:2), the end of all things; but before that, there is a *personal* Eschaton that can be realized, where a person undergoes some final-Eschaton-like phenomena, such as seeing GOD, also perhaps in the fashion of 1 John 3:2, but where this happens before the final Eschaton at the end of the world.

So, in summary, we are referring to the following two ways of considering the Eschaton event, both of which are 1 John 3:2-level events:

1. Personal Eschaton: "the end of the world"[1] as direct revelation of GOD, revealing that this world is passing away (1 John 2:17), containing the

---

1. I am using the phrase "end of the world" much in the way that it is used in this verse:

> For then must he often have suffered since the foundation of the world: but now once in the end of the world hath he appeared to put away sin by the sacrifice of himself. (Heb 9:26)

In this verse, "end of the world" appears to be more in line with how we have defined the personal Eschaton versus the Eschaton (final Eschaton), where it is not only the time of the sky splitting into the end of all things of the closing of the timeline of the physical world, but further, in Heb 9:26 the end of the world is about a realization of the crucified

realization of the final Eschaton, including the mind residing, in some way, in the future, in the afterlife, partially, rather than only in the physical existence, despite body and mind continuing to exist before the state of bodily death (for example, Saul on the Damascus Road).

2. Eschaton (also called the *final* Eschaton): "the end of the world" in the future, as the time of the splitting of the sky (see Luke 20:34–36), to see GOD directly (Rev 1:7), leading into the end of all things (1 Pet 4:7).

It is important to outline these two Eschaton events in this book, since we will see below that they are both vividly described in Scripture. Every person will *see* the Eschaton, but only the chosen will see the personal Eschaton, which is before the Eschaton (the final Eschaton).

Eschaton-like events in Scripture often replicate and build (Feeding of the Four Thousand, and of the Five Thousand, etc.). For example, in Exodus we see an earlier, much smaller-scale Eschaton-like event, when Moses meets with GOD on Mount Sinai (Exod 19:17–20), with many of the same signs and revelations as found for the entire world later in Revelation. Such Eschaton-like repetitions and foreshadowings of the events leading up to the Eschaton, events mimicking the Eschaton, are quite widespread phenomena in Scripture. It is as if the Eschaton is being felt and lived, in some ways, pervasively, in the present and *before* the Eschaton. Perhaps this repeating and building Eschaton offers some hint of an explanation of verses such as these:

> Again, a new commandment I write unto you, which thing is true in him and in you: because the darkness is past, and the true light now shineth. (1 John 2:8)

> I have overthrown some of you, as God overthrew Sodom and Gomorrah, and ye were as a firebrand plucked out of the burning: yet have ye not returned unto me, saith the Lord. Therefore thus will I do unto thee, O Israel: and because I will do this unto thee, prepare to meet thy God, O Israel. (Amos 4:11–12)

By this, we can see how the theology in Hyper-Calvinist universal salvation reveals how important it is for a person to be talking to GOD (verbally or nonverbally), where there is an interaction with him by him hearing us.

GOD and his cross that saves.

Bibliography

Balfour, Walter. A*n Inquiry the Scriptural Import of the Words Sheol, Hades, Tartarus, and Gehenna: All Translated Hell, in the Common English Version.* Charleston, MA: George Davidson, 1825.

Chisholm, Roderick. *On Metaphysics.* Minneapolis: University of Minnesota Press, 1989.

Crisp, Oliver D. *Deviant Calvinism: Broadening Reformed Theology.* Minneapolis: Fortress, 2014.

Davies, Paul. *Superforce: The Search for a Grand Unified Theory of Nature.* New York: Simon & Schuster. 1984

Dowden, Bradley. "Zeno's Paradoxes." *Internet Encyclopedia of Philosophy.* ISSN 2161-0002. https://iep.utm.edu/zenos-paradoxes/.

Ehrman, Bart D. "The History of Heaven and Hell." Smith-Pettit Lecture presented at the Sunstone Digital Symposium, July 29, 2020. Video recording. https://www.youtube.com/watch?v=L_eZf33UMs8. Copyright © Bart D. Ehrman and Sunstone Education Foundation.

Grupp, Jeff. "Why God Did Not Choose All Souls: New Scriptural Evidence." *Philosophy and Theology* 32 (2020) 93–117.

———. *GOD-Faith: Discovering the Pure Logic Built into the Fabric of Reality.* Self-published through BookBaby, 2019.

Hesslink, John. "The Revelation of God in Creation and Scripture: Calvin's Theology and Its Early Reception." In *Calvin's Theology and Its Reception: Disputes, Developments, and New Possibilities,* edited by J. Todd Billings and John Hesslink, 3–24. Louisville: Westminster John Knox, 2012.

Kane, Gordon. *Supersymmetry: Squarks, Photinos, and the Unveiling of the Ultimate Laws of Nature.* Cambridge, MA: Perseus, 2000.

Karamanolis, George. *The Philosophy of Early Christianity.* New York: Routledge, 2014.

Launonen, Lari. "Hell and the Cultural Evolution of Christianity." *Theology and Science* 20 (2022) 19–208.

Lenchack, Timothy A. "What's Biblical about . . . Hell?" *Bible Today* 51 (2013) 116–17.

MacDonald, Gregory. *The Evangelical Universalist.* 2nd ed. Eugene, OR: Cascade. 2012.

Searle, John R. *The Mystery of Consciousness.* New York: New York Review Books, 1997.

Toon, Peter. *The Emergence of Hyper-Calvinism in English Nonconformity 1689–1765.* Eugene, OR: Wipf & Stock, 2011.

Van Inwagen, Peter. "The Powers of Rational Beings: Freedom of the Will." In *Philosophy: The Quest for Truth,* edited by Louis P. Pojman, 429–44. 8th ed. New York: Oxford University Press, 2012.

Subject Index

Achilles, Paradox of (Zeno of Elea), 118
Adam and Eve, Scripture does not mention any perfection involved with, 136
agnosticism, 13
all flesh seeing GOD/Christ directly at the Eschaton, 7, 15-16, 35, 60, 74, 94-96, 123, 142
all in all, Christ is, 80, 93
all men are sinners, 10
all sins forgiven (by GOD), 17
all things new, 43, 116
all things opened and exposed to GOD, 93
alternate reality after the Mark of the Beast, 94
amazed while burning in the Lake of Fire, 83, 97, 126, 128
angels (humans becoming in the afterlife), 29, 54, 73
antichrist, 14, 93
antinomian, Hyper-Calvinism is, 7
astrophysics, 17
atheism, 13
atonement, 78
Augustinian universalism, 7
awakened in the grave by the voice of the LORD, 19-20, 26, 31, 59, 90, 117, 119, 141

backward causation (GOD pulling all to the Eschaton), 141
Baptism of Fire, 5-6, 51, 54, 68, 73, 121-129
beheaded reign with Christ for a Thousand Years, 91

being swallowed, consumed, by GOD, 84-85, 88, 121
birth pangs of the last days, 77
blinded from having understanding of Scripture, 2, 40, 69
blocked (by GOD) from believing in GOD, 53
body of Christ (is all people), 130
burning in hell, people, 2, 54, 63, 69
Byzantine Majority, 61

Calvin, John, and the dictation view of Scripture, 36
Chisholm, Roderick (American philosopher), 42
chosen and unchosen, 54, 57, 59, 90-91
Christ dying for the ungodly (saving us as sinners), 17, 34-35, 139
chronons (atoms of time), 42
clay vessels, 66
Codex Vaticanus, 69
coinherent time (during the Great Tribulation and Thousand Years), 92-94
coinherence with GOD, 6, 36, 80, 84, 92
condemned all raised at the Eschaton, the, 70-71, 73, 90
confessing the Name (as being what the salvific do), 14
Consuming Fire (GOD), 1, 2, 4-5, 7-8, 17, 50, 51, 62, 73-75, 79-80, 82-83, 85, 94, 98, 114-115, 121-123, 127, 141
continuous time, philosophy of, 42

Subject Index

contradictions supposedly in the Bible solved by Hyper-Calvinist universal salvation, 1, 3, 13, 17, 33, 40, 48, 63, 99
corrupted things, GOD only creates, 50, 78, 120, 136–139
creatio ex nihilo, 50, 65, 116
Crisp, Oliver, 7
cross, metaphysics and perfect logic of the, 74, 119

Damascus Road, 82, 143
Date, Chris (contemporary pre-Eschaton annihilation theologian), 19, 60
Davies, Paul (Australian physicist), 116
days of Noah and time near Eschaton resembling one another, 10, 34
dead all raised, the, 54, 72, 84–85, 89, 94
dead in Christ, 89
death and hell cease to exist, 2–3, 72–73
death assimilated into, digested by, GOD, 77, 85
death cast into the Lake of Fire, 71
death of death (Rev 20:14), 51, 53–54, 69, 70–73, 76, 86–87, 90, 97
death has no power over them, 97
death shall be destroyed (at the Eschaton), the last enemy, 69, 78, 87
death swallowed up, consumed, 74, 77, 78, 84–85, 88–90, 121
deductive syllogism, 68
Descension of GOD at the Eschaton to save the condemned, 1, 5, 7, 77, 91, 96, 132
deviant Calvinism, 7
dictation view of Scripture, 3, 36
disembodied consciousness, 26
dormancy of the soul (pre-Eschaton), 28
double predestination, Hyper-Calvinist, 59, 116

ecstatic Fire, GOD as, 6
ecstatic presence of GOD, 8

ecstatic theology, 80
end of all things, 4–5, 10, 16, 24, 44, 68, 75, 82, 96, 142, 143
Ehrman, Bart, 39
Eschaton as great attractor, 16–17
Eschaton awakening of dormant soul and/or nonexistent self, 26
Eschaton cloud-cover (anomalous clouds at the Eschaton), 89, 91, 141
Eschaton, differing levels of, and timing of, 142
Eschaton Fire felt/experienced before the Eschaton, 16, 34, 51–52, 58–59, 92, 141, 143
Eschaton revelation changes corrupt things to incorrupt, 81, 84
eternal conscious torment (by GOD), 4
eternal conscious torment in hell, 63, 67–68, 88
eternal fire, 38, 114–115
eternal security, 35
everlasting and/or eternal punishment, 17, 25, 36, 38–41, 43–44, 64, 99
everlasting contempt, 27, 112
everlasting destruction, 36
Everlasting Fire (is GOD, Lake of Fire), 44, 109
every knee shall bow, every tongue shall confess, 14–16, 58
evil as distinct from sin, 138
evil, GOD creates, 138
extreme Calvinism, 8

false eschatology, 11
fiery over (in Scripture), 85
first resurrection, 71, 91, 101
five-point Calvinism, 8
flashing in and out of existence (all quantum particles, all physical reality), 116
forever, being condemned, 99
forever (condemnation as forever) as a hole in time, 100–105
forever is three days (Jonah 2), 100–102
forever, pre-Eschaton annihilation as eternal and, 25, 99–100

Subject Index

forever, types of, 103
fractality of Scripture, 34, 143
fractality of time, 92–94, 101–102
Francis of Assisi (Saint), 8, 82
free will choice (as an entity not created by God), 12, 120
free will choice (as not scriptural), human, 7–9, 15, 63, 66, 68, 135
free will of GOD, 65
free will theology, 53
furnace, the, 56

garden of Eden, 51, 139
Gehenna, 99, 105, 109–110, 114
gnashing of teeth, 56–57
goats burned in the Lake of Fire, 38, 53, 111
GOD can only interact with humans as sinners (pre-Eschaton), 134, 138–140
GOD's presence, 34, 121–130
GOD's presence (separated from due to pre-Eschaton self-annihilation/self-nonexistence), 40
GOD revealed in-full at the Eschaton, 83
GOD revealed in nature (tenet of Hyper-Calvinism), 8
greatest conceivable Being, GOD as the, 13, 50
Great Tribulation, 92, 142

Hades, 2, 4, 26, 39, 49, 58, 63, 67, 69, 86, 105
heathen reconciled with GOD, 70
heavens and earth burn with fire (at the Eschaton) and pass away, the, 3–5, 24, 82–83
hell as aspect of pre-Eschaton annihilation, 24
hell does exist, 8
hell, GOD with people when they are in, 117
hell is not forever (destroyed at the Eschaton), 44, 58, 64, 70 , 87, 97, 99–108, 109

hell, people being removed/released from, cast out of, 22, 69, 73, 77, 110
hell versus Hades, 26–27
Hitler, Adolf, 2. 63–64
horizontal infinity, horizontal time (unending), 100, 102–105, 115–116
Hort and Westcott, 61, 69
Hyper-Calvinism, 1–3,
Hyper-Calvinist universal salvation, definition of, 7–8
Hyperreality, 94
hyper-sovereignty of GOD (in Hyper-Calvinism), 8, 116
hyperspace, infinite (as all realities coinhereing with Christ/GOD), 93

image of Christ, 27
imitation of Christ, 74
inerrantism, scriptural, 2,
infinite dimensions, 36
infinite love of GOD, 3, 77, 120, 140
Infinite Spirit, GOD as, 13, 40
inner mind created by GOD, 65
Innermost Fire, GOD's being is, 73, 122
Innermostness of GOD interacting with innermostness of humans, 123
inner self as real self (more predominantly than body as self), 29–30, 122
inside of GOD before time (Eccl 12:7), 131
intermediate state, the (rapture), 91
introspective confirmation of salvation in Hyper-Calvinism, 7–8

jail ministry, 13, 132
Jesus is the crucified GOD, 17, 74, 82,4, 134
judgment of GOD defined, 72

Kane, Gordon (American physicist), 116
Kant, Immanuel, 20
Kingdom of GOD reaches all, 55
kingdom of the sun, 56

Subject Index

King James Bible, 2,

Lake of Fire and GOD do the same tasks, 75–76,
Lake of Fire as baptism, 91, 97
Lake of Fire ends death, 74, 97
Lake of Fire, full intensity of, 90, 96
Lake of Fire, GOD is the, 2–5, 68
Lake of Fire is the Refiner's Fire (GOD), 121–129
Lake of Fire, salvation inside of, 54, 78
Lake of Fire, transcends all things, 5
land of the dead, 67, 101, 105, 115
last trumpet (when death is destroyed), 78, 88–90, 94, 96
Laurentian, Saint (martyrdom), 82
let this cup pass from me, 66
light (humans shining, in the afterlife), 53
lightning of GOD, 114
limited atonement paradox, the, 48
literalist/hyper-literalist interpretation of Scripture, 3, 6, 8, 19, 48, 92–94, 113

mark of the beast, 91–94
martyrdom, 21–22, 82, 91
meeting Christ in the clouds, 91
mercy on all, GOD having, 72
mind as spirit, 106
mind transplant, 30
Mount Sinai, 102, 143
no more tears (at the Eschaton), 73–76, 77, 98
not remembering the former things (after the Eschaton), 47, 77
Ocean of Fire (parallel to Days of Noah), 10, 75, 83–85, 88
omnicausality / occasionalism, 3, 8, 116
omni-coinherence of all realities in GOD, 93
one fold (humanity as one flock with one GOD), 55, 57
oneness with Christ/GOD, 88
only GOD can end, conquer, swallow death, 74, 76
overcoming death, 27, 74

Parable of the Tares, 52, 53–57, 76, 111
paradise, 105
people (sinners) cast into the Lake of Fire after death is destroyed, 87–88
perfect and infinite logic of Scripture, 13, 40
pit, the, 99, 103–105, 115
Plank time, 116
Poerete, Margarette, 18
popular and traditional (non-scriptural) theology, contradictions in, 13
preach the Gospel to every creature, 133
pre-Eschaton annihilation as being under the ocean, 21, 100, 117
pre-Eschaton annihilation as bringing one immediately to the Eschaton, 21–22
pre-Eschaton annihilation as freedom, 22–23
pre-Eschaton annihilation as forever, eternal, 25, 28
pre-Eschaton annihilation as *inevitable* gap, fissure, for old self to cease, and afterlife self to commence, 24–26, 28–29, 100–102, 105–106
pre-Eschaton annihilation as sleep or fainting, 24–26, 100, 108
pre-Eschaton annihilation as temporary destruction of self, 24–26
pre-Eschaton annihilation as underworldly, 28–29, 31, 36–37, 106, 116–117, 119
pre-Eschaton annihilation caused by the presence of GOD, 37
pre-Eschaton annihilation theology compared to post-Eschaton annihilation theology, 18–20
pre-Eschaton annihilation, types of, 18, 101
post-Eschaton annihilation as non-scriptural, inconsistent theology, 19, 27–28, 70
post-thingness, 133
problem of evil (solved), 135–140

Subject Index

qualia, 23, 26, 101, 130
quantum annihilation, 116
quantum physics, 116

rapture into a place of hiding, 77, 91-92
rapture (pre-tribulation) as being body death (deliverance), 91, 94
rapture, pre-Tribulation, 77, 94
rapturing at the start of the Eschaton, 90
reality, higher order of, 5
rejection of sound doctrine, 11
resurrection of self at the Eschaton, 25-31, 43, 88, 94
restoration and reconciliation of all things (by GOD), 5, 6, 54, 58, 84, 136, 139, 141

salt at salvation, 113
salted with Fire, everyone is, 34, 113
salvation can only happen via GOD's infinite love, 120, 140
salvation via immolation in GOD, 2, 5-6, 34, 50-51, 68, 73, 81, 83-84, 88, 90, 95-96, 116
Satan's first sin, 139-40
saved by Fire of GOD (Consuming Fire, Lake of Fire), 10-11, 21, 98
Searl, John (American philosopher), 106
seas and rivers drying up, 93
second death, the, 54, 68-69, 76, 82, 88, 95, 97
second resurrection, 73, 82, 84, 88
seeing GOD face-to-face, 17
seeing GOD pre-Eschaton (through a glass darkly), 22, 51, 124, 133
self (annihilated self) recreated at the Eschaton, 28, 41-43
self defined as stream of consciousness, 20, 23, 29-30, 118-119
self haecceity (gaps within), 23, 26-29, 41-43, 100, 106
serving the poorest (in Hyper-Calvinism), 8
Sheol, 67, 99, 105

simpleton hyper-literalist approach to Scripture, 3, 13
sin as nothingness (uncreated hole of nonexistence inside the human soul), 138-139
sin, GOD creates all things but does not create, 138
sky splitting at the Eschaton, 142
soul destruction/nonexistence, 24, 26, 30-31
spirit saved and body destroyed/burned at the Eschaton, 1, 7, 27, 68, 73, 98, 133
stars falling, 93
Stehpen's martyrdom (Acts 6-7), 21-22
stigmata of Francis of Assisi, 82
sun brightening during the final days, 93, 114
suns (humans and GOD being like suns in the afterlife), 53, 56-57
Supralapsarianism, 7, 35
systematic theology, 3,

talking to GOD, 143
Textus Receptus, 2, 60, 69, 111
thief in the night, 92
There shall be no more death, 70, 73, 76
thousand years is a day, a, 92
Thousand Years, the, 91-98
the Thousand Years as alternate reality, 93
time, alternative philosophy of (during the 1000 years), 58-59, 92-93
time as number line (Real numbers), 103, 118
time stoppage (vertical infinity of pre-Eschaton annihilation), 103, 105, 118-119
time-warping, 94
torturing people, GOD (supposedly), 4, 17, 54, 110-111
traditional and popular view of hell (defined), 12
traditional view and popular of hell (as a doctrine of devils), 12
traditional view and popular of hell as logical contradiction, 13

Subject Index

traditional view and popular of hell concept turning people from Christianity, 12–13
tyrant, GOD as (in traditional Calvinism, non-Hyper-Calvinism), 119

uncountable infinity (vertical inifinty), 118
unearned salvation, 7
unicorns descending during the final days, 93
universal salvation of humanity as being *life* (in Christ), 9
Valley of Hinnon, 67
vertical infinity as pre-Eschaton annihilation, 102, 105–106, 112, 115–116

waiting during pre-Eschaton rapture, 91–92
waiting for the LORD (all creation groaning), 84
wanting to save all (as identical to where he will save all), GOD, 61
why GOD did not choose all souls before the Eschaton, 26, 33, 50, 72
world burned by Fire, entire, 75, 99
world reserved for Fire, 141
wrath of GOD (associated with the rapture), 85, 91, 142

Zeno of Elea (ancient Greek philosopher), 115–116, 118–19

Scripture Index

GENESIS
1	137
1-3	136
2:7	131
6:9	137
32:30	102

EXODUS
3:1-6	75
19:17-20	143
12:10-13	3, 7, 10
20-21	125-126

NUMBERS
31	125
31:23	124, 126

DEUTERONOMY
4:12	75
4:24	75, 121
4:36	6, 111, 122-123
5:4-6	123
5:22-26	74
5:22-28	124
5:24	73, 75
7:6	35
9:3	75
24	75
29:23	113
32:22	111, 129
32:39	74

JUDGES
9:23	140

1 SAMUEL
16:7	29, 107, 123
16:14-16	140
28	26

2 SAMUEL
22:31	81

1 KINGS
19	79

JOB
1:1	137
5	43
7	43
10-15	43
14:1-4	43
16:10	118
26:6	122

PSALM
2:27	117
13	107
13:3	20
16:10	117, 119
21:9	85
23:4	64
32:1-2	140
33:13-15	122

Scripture Index

(Psalm continued)

37:20	129
39	19
39:11-13	19, 22-23, 119
46	16
46:2-3	16
49:15	76
66:10-12	124
79:11	81, 85, 118
84:11	53
86:13	67
88	21-22
88:1-7	21
29:1	85
88:5	29
90:8	122
90:3	106
92:7	25
100:3	120
115:16-18	97
115:3	29, 61, 65-66,
116:11	3, 6, 125
117:1	52
139:8	39
139:7-17	117
139:7-8	107
139:8	117
145:7	120
146:1-4	23
147:5	134
150	17
150:6	8, 16

PROVERBS

3:5-6	81
9:10	81
15:11	122
16:4	85

ECCLESIASTES

3:11	2, 132
9:5	97
12:7	54, 105, 122, 131

ISAIAH

1:28	25
2:2-3	92
6:9-10	48
9:2	53
13:8-9	127
13:8	6, 73, 77, 85, 98, 126, 128
13:6-9	126-127
13:6-8	83
13:6	127
14:15	104
19:13-14	140
19:5-6	93
25:8-26:19	76
25:6-9	74, 75-78
25:8	69, 74-75, 78, 84, 121
25:6-9	77
25:6-8	91
25:7	2
25	77, 79
26:15-21	92
26:20-21	77
26:18-20	93
26:15	92
26:11	77
26:17-20	22
26:19	27, 77
26:18	77
26:20	142
26:12	66
26:17-20	
26:16-17	77
26:17	137
26:7-11	73
26	77
30:26	93
31:7	60
34:7	93
34:2	32
40:5	4, 7, 17, 60, 142
40:4-5	16
43:25	132
43:18-19	5
45:23	15
45:7	138
48:9-11	124
48:10	129
49:26	15-16
55:8	2
59:2	80

65:24	141
65:17	48
66:23	60
66:14-24	96-97
66:15-17	35
66:15-16	75
66:15	4-5,
66	96

JEREMIAH

5:8	80
18:4	34, 66, 137, 139

LAMENTATIONS

3:29-32	70
3:31	60
37	93, 96

EZEKIEL

8:2-4	6
14:5	80
28:17	139-140
36:27	64
38:20	16

DANIEL

2:43	66
7:7-9	6
11:45-12:3	91
11:36-37	93
12:2-3	53, 111
12:1-2	77, 91
12:2	27

HOSEA

6:1-3	106
13:13-14	77

JOEL

2:32	14
2:28	7

AMOS

4:11-12	118

9:11-15	70
9:3	107

JONAH

2:6-7	100
2:1-2	107
2:7	22, 107
2:6	25, 103, 104, 113
2:4	107
2:2	107
2	21, 27, 77, 100, 103, 104, 117, 119

HABAKKUK

1:13	13

ZEPH

1:17	2
3:8-9	11

ZECHARIAH

3:2	118
9:11	81, 118
13:8-9	118, 129
13:9	124

MALACHI

3:1-3	124
3:3	124
3:2	125
4:2	53
4:1	4

MATTHEW

1:18	89
2:1	89
3:11	73, 125, 131-133
5:30	113
5:13-16	113
5:13	113
7:13-14	7, 9
9:24	31
10:28	24, 39, 106, 108
11:27	34
11:25	73

Scripture Index

(Matthew continued)

12:34	122
12:43	37
13:33	52, 55
13:24-43	56
13:10-15	56
13	52
15:22	37
17:2	53
18:8-9	109-110
18	110
22:30	129
22:14	33, 51
24:27	37, 114
24:46	38-39
24:35	4-5, 10
24:31	92
24:7-8	127
25:40-46	44
25:46	38-39,
25:41	38, 41, 44
25	38-39, 44
26:39	66
27:52	93
28:18	34
28:3	114

MARK

1:37	17
3:28	14, 17, 132
4:11-12	2-3
4:12	48, 53
9:49-50	62
9:49	4, 34, 50, 62, 102, 113-114
9:48	114
9:43-50	112, 114
9:43-48	115
12:25-27	27
13:31	24, 58, 109, 121
13:3	4-5
16:15	8, 133

LUKE

2:25-30	9
2:8-12	58
3:16	73, 89, 125, 131, 133
3:5-6	16
3:6	4, 16, 142
3:5	16
6:20	8
8:50-55	31
8:10	48
10:15	8, 69
11:39-40	20, 26, 65-66, 119-120, 124, 133
12:49	4, 52, 111
14:12-15	8
16:23	111
16:19-31	46
16:16	52
16:1-13	47
17:24	35, 114
17:5	133
20:37-38	54
20:34-36	73, 143
20:38	54
20:36	5, 29, 54, 129
20:34-36	142
21:33	24
24:46	27

JOHN

1:29	14, 59
1:13	122, 131
1:9	17, 51, 122-124
1:5	117
3:35	34
3:30	133
3:17-18	1
3:18	72
3:17	81
4:24	81, 133
4:10	9
5:28-29	26, 34, 90
5:28	51
5:25-29	19, 89
5:25-28	19-20, 59
5:25	34, 123, 141-142
5:24	114
6:63	29, 122
6:44	132
6:39	34
6:33	52, 60
9:39	2
10:11-17	58

10:16	55, 58, 64, 71	8:38-39	39-40, 107, 117
10:6-9	58	8:22-23	59
10:1-4	58	8:21-23	52
10	55, 57-58	8:23	84
11:25	54	8:19	17
11:11-14	31	9:19-23	66
12:40	2	10:9-10	14
12:32	16-17, 55, 123, 132-133, 141	11:36	79
14:6	9	11:33-34	72
15:13	140	11:32	51, 72
15:5	3, 66, 81, 93, 116, 124, 137	11:30	72
16:33	131	11	72
17:3	15-16	14:23	140
17:2	34	14:11-13	15
		14:10-11	15
		14:8	54
		14	15

ACTS

2:27-29	67
2:27	32, 118
2:23	8
2	6, 131
3:21	5-6, 17, 54, 58-59, 81, 84, 121, 139, 141
7:54-60	31
7:60	22
7:56	22
7	91
6:7	133
6-7	22
17:30-31	72
17:28	81
24:15	27

ROMANS

1:20	79
3:12	72
3:10	10
3:4	3, 125
4:8	137
4:6	7
5:18	9, 59-60
5:15	9
5:11	6
5:6-8	139
5:6	17
6:23	9
6:19-20	35
6	

1 CORINTHIANS

1:21	125
1:18	2
1:2	72
3:14-15	10
3:13-15	59
3:12-15	1-2, 7, 68, 84, 88, 129
3:15	3, 50-51, 95
3:13	35
3:12	22, 34,
4:5	34, 60
5:5-6	27
5:4-5	128
5:5	1, 37, 54, 68, 72-73, 79, 98, 128, 133-34
6:17	78
8:6	79
12:23	131
12:11-13	131
13:12	51, 124
15:54	88, 90
15:52	50, 72, 84
15:51	79
15:51-54	90
15:50-55	78
15:50	129
15:42-44	84, 136
15:42	28, 48, 50, 55, 79-80, 136-37
15:24-26	69

Scripture Index

(1 Corinthians continued)

15:23-24	10
15:26	73, 78
15:22	9, 60
15:20-22	27
15:13-14	66
15	84

2 CORINTHIANS

4:3-4	2
5:19	58
5:18	79
5:17	5, 28, 101
5:10	72
5:8	67
12:9	110
12:1-4	26

GALATIANS

2:20	54, 78, 101
2:17	138-39
3:28	130

EPHESIANS

1:4	50, 102, 123
1:23	79-81, 93, 107, 124, 141
1:10	71
4:30	35
4:4-6	71
4:6	124

PHILIPPIANS

1:6	66, 137
2:2	131
2:10-11	15
3:21	54
4:7	5

COLOSSIANS

1:20-22	4, 54
1:20	58, 84, 136
2:2	134
2:19	133
3:11	71, 81, 130

1 THESSALONIANS

2:19	52
4:14-18	89, 91
4:16-17	88, 94
4:15	25
4	90

2 THESSALONIANS

1:7-10	36
1:7-9	16
1:7	75, 82
1:9	25, 40, 80
2:4	93

1 TIMOTHY

2:3-4	7, 10-11
2:4	60-61
4:10	61
4:1	12
6:16	102

2 TIMOTHY

1:9-10	76

TITUS

2:11	17

HEBREWS

1:10-12	52
1:7	129
2:17	74, 119
2:11	78-79, 132
4:13	93, 122
6:13	13
6:9	61
9:26	142
12:29	4, 50, 75, 1:21

JAMES

2:26	31
2:13	72

Scripture Index

1 PETER

1:17	72
2:9	35
4:12-14	131
4:7	4-5, 16, 24, 44, 68, 75, 96, 121, 142-43

2 PETER

1:4	130
3:10-12	75
3:12	4-5
3:10	24, 82, 92, 109
3:7-8	92, 141
3:6-9	10
3:6-7	75
3:8	92-93
3:7	4, 111, 123
3	75

1 JOHN

2:17	142
2:8	143
2:2	14, 17, 59, 132
3:4	138
3:2	6-7, 17, 22, 34-35, 42, 51, 53, 78, 81-82, 85, 95, 130, 132, 142
4:15	14
4:7-9	40
4:7-8	4, 120
4:2-3	14

2 JOHN

1:7	14

REVELATION

1:7	7, 51, 142-43
2:11	51, 62, 98, 141
4:11	65-66, 81, 120
5:13	51
6:13-14	93
6:12	93
6:20	16
6:14	16
8:5	114
11:19	114
13:15-18	93
13:16	92
16:18	93, 114
17	94
19:6	133
20:15	75, 87
20:14-15	52, 86
20:14	2-5, 14, 58, 67, 69, 70-75, 78-79, 81, 84, 86-88, 105, 117
20:13	8, 26, 69, 70, 72-73, 77, 86-87, 110
20:12-14	71-72
20:12-13	73
20:11-15	75
20:10-14	83
20:10	109
20:9-13	83
20:7-14	83
20:7-9	79, 83
20:6	62, 91, 141
20:5	19, 91, 93-94
20:5-6	71-73
20:4-6	19, 91, 94, 97, 101
20:4	92
20	2, 71, 77, 82, 96
20:14-21:6	76-77
21:8	53-54, 75, 87-88, 98, 98
21:5	5, 43, 116
21:4	70, 73, 98
21:1-6	76
21:1-3	86
21:1	24, 75
21	2, 71, 77, 83, 96, 98
22:5	54
22:3-5	105

www.ingramcontent.com/pod-product-compliance
Lightning Source LLC
Chambersburg PA
CBHW051939160426
43198CB00013B/2223